THE CHRISTIAN AND Alcoholic Beverages

THE CHRISTIAN AND

Alcoholic Beverages

A Biblical Perspective

KENNETH L. GENTRY, JR.

BAKER BOOK HOUSE
Grand Rapids, Michigan 49506

ISBN: 0-8010-3807-3

Printed in the United States of America

Unless otherwise noted Scripture quotations are from the New American Standard
Bible, © The Lockman Foundation 1960, 1962, 1963, 1968, 1971, 1972, 1973,
1975, 1977.

To my wife
Melissa
who first encouraged me to expand my ministry
through publication

Contents

Foreword

The biblical doctrine of the sufficiency of Holy Scripture, as set forth in the creeds and confessions of the early church and recaptured at the time of the Protestant Reformation, has suffered in the twentieth century at the hands of some of its staunchest defenders. This has perhaps been most apparent as Christians seek guidance in matters of ethical concern, such as in the use of or abstention from alcoholic beverages.

The apostle Paul, writing under the inspiration of the Holy Spirit, was not remiss in passing over the so-called "arguments of common sense." Such arguments are frequently advanced in favor of a "more acceptable" interpretation than what a normal reading of Scripture alone would produce. Would it be realistic for the apostle to exhort Timothy to teach, rebuke, correct, and train in righteousness, depending on God's Word alone, if it were not adequate and completely sufficient in itself? Is the man of God "thoroughly equipped for every good work" if he must depend on the ever-changing cultural mores and traditions often set forth by segments of the Christian community seeking to bind his conscience more perfectly? (Read 2 Timothy 3:14–17.)

Kenneth Gentry believes the Scriptures are sufficient in themselves to be a reliable and trustworthy guide for the Christian . . . even in today's highly complex society. In his book Gentry examines the entire alcoholic beverage issue and related problems facing people of all ages in our churches today. Both Old and New Testament materials are painstakingly exegeted as Gentry seeks to draw out the teaching of the Bible. Especially illuminating and helpful is the handling of frequently raised objections to his conclusions.

While the entire book is probably the best treatment of the "moderation viewpoint" that I have read, the chapters on the weak and strong brethren and the stumbling block offer really practical help for most readers. But it was the brief chapter on the "potential alcoholic" that was, to me, the one smooth stone in David's sling that killed the giant argument so often used by Christians committed to the total abstinence viewpoint.

The church of Jesus Christ must regain a fresh sense of awareness and understanding that the Holy Scriptures are completely trustworthy to guide Christians through difficult problems and situations. Synods and general assemblies need to consider Kenneth Gentry's book and seek unity on this important question; individuals need a handbook of reference as they face this question in their daily lives.

This is a controversial book. However, Gentry's accurate scholarship and irenic spirit is evident, even in those sensitive areas that crop up throughout the study. In my opinion this book is a safe choice to hand to anyone interested in this subject, even to someone who may hold strongly to an opposing viewpoint.

And finally, I sincerely believe that Kenneth Gentry has written a book that honors our Lord Jesus Christ. Consequently, I believe that its publication at this time will significantly advance and strengthen Christ's Kingdom.

Walter C. Hibbard, Founder and President
Puritan Reformed Discount Book Service
Wilmington, Delaware

Abbreviations for Notes

Arndt-Gingrich   W. F. Arndt and F. W. Gingrich, A Greek-English
                         Lexicon of the New Testament (Chicago: University of
                         Chicago Press, 1957).

Brown-Driver-Briggs Francis Brown, S. R. Driver, and Charles A.
                         Briggs, A Hebrew and English Lexicon of the Old
                         Testament (Oxford: Clarendon Press, 1972 ed.).

Friedrich, TDNT   Gerhard Friedrich, Theological Dictionary of the New
                         Testament (Grand Rapids: Eerdmans, 1971).

Gilchrist   Paul R. Gilchrist, ed., "Study Committee on
                         Beverage Use of Alcohol Report" in Documents of
                         Synod (Lookout Mtn., TN: Reformed Presbyterian
                         Church, Evangelical Synod, 1982).

ISBE   James Orr, ed., International Standard Bible
                         Encyclopedia (Grand Rapids: Eerdmans, rep. 1956).

Kittel, TDNT   Gerhard Kittel, Theological Dictionary of the New
                         Testament (Grand Rapids: Eerdmans, 1967).

Lindsell   Harold Lindsell, The World, the Flesh and the Devil
                         (Washington: Canon Press, 1973).

O'Brien-Chafetz   Robert O'Brien and Morris Chafetz, M.D., The
                         Encyclopedia of Alcoholism (New York: Facts on File,
                         1982).

Reynolds   Stephen M. Reynolds, Alcohol and the Bible (Little
                         Rock: The Challenge Press, 1983).

Thayer   Joseph Henry Thayer, A Greek-English Lexicon of the
                         New Testament (New York: American Book Co.,
                         1889).

11

1

Introductory Matters

There are few issues of practice that continually tend to resurface in the stream of Christianity more likely to stir deep-seated feelings and generate more heated debate than the Christian view of alcoholic beverages. This issue has divided Christians "in sundry times and divers manners." During the course of American history, the matter has not only been debated in virtually every branch of Christendom, but has resulted in actions ranging from educational temperance movements within Christian circles to constitutional prohibition in society at large.

The Issue Before Us

Basically there are three classic positions that have been taken on the question of drink. In the present work these will be called the prohibitionist, the abstentionist, and the moderationist views.

The *prohibitionist* position maintains that alcoholic beverages are to be universally avoided as unfit for human consumption and specifically forbidden by Scripture. Some prohibitionists regard alcoholic beverages themselves to be inherently evil.[1] Others deem the act of partaking them to be immoral. Representative of this latter and more standard view is Stephen M. Reynolds's *Alcohol and the Bible*.[2] In this view the question of alcohol is a "legal" matter—it is forbidden by the law of God.

1. David Wilkerson, *Sipping Saints* (Old Tappan, NJ: Spire Books, 1979).
2. Stephen M. Reynolds, *Alcohol and the Bible* (Little Rock: Challenge Press, 1983). See also Ernest Gordon, *Christ, the Apostles, and Wine* (Nashville: Sunday School Times, 1944).

The *abstentionist* view maintains that although alcoholic beverages are not expressly forbidden in Scripture as a matter of universal practice, alcohol consumption in our society is nevertheless imprudent and should not be condoned. This is due to both the moral-social context in which we live and the easy availability of highly alcoholic (distilled) beverages. Representative of this view is the position published by the (former) Reformed Presbyterian Church, Evangelical Synod, in "Study Committee on the Beverage Use of Alcohol Report."[3] In this view, abstinence is not a matter of "law," but of love. Thus it is to be voluntarily given up as a matter of prudence.[4]

The *moderationist* view maintains that alcoholic beverages are permissible to Christians if moderately consumed and in a circumspect manner. Representative of this view is G. I. Williamson's *Wine in the Bible and the Church.*[5] This is the view endorsed by the present writer.

The issue before us is an important one that merits due consideration by concerned Christians. The implications of the question are many and varied. We will briefly allude to three by way of introduction to the study.

First, the issue has important ramifications for both the individual's personal witness and his Christian counsel. As redeemed vessels of mercy (1 Cor. 6:19–20; Titus 2:11–14), Christians are obligated to strive self-consciously to live out every aspect of their lives to the glory of God (1 Cor. 10:31; Col. 3:17). Given the fact that the alcohol question will not simply go away, the Christian should be ready to give a biblical answer to any who may inquire into his position and practice in regard to drink. This may be done either to defend or to enhance

---

3. Paul R. Gilchrist, ed., "Study Committee on Beverage Use of Alcohol Report" in *Documents of Synod* (Lookout Mtn., TN: Reformed Presbyterian Church, Evangelical Synod, 1982), pp. 19–33. See also Harold Lindsell, *The World, the Flesh and the Devil* (Washington: Canon Press, 1973), chapter 8.

4. See the distinction made here by Gleason L. Archer, *Encyclopedia of Bible Difficulties* (Grand Rapids: Zondervan, 1982), p. 149.

5. G. I. Williamson, *Wine in the Bible and the Church* (Phillipsburg, NJ: Pilgrim Pub. Co., 1976). See also: J. G. Vos, *The Separated Life* (Philadelphia: Great Commission Publications).

one's Christian witness. Or it may be done to provide a biblically based counsel to those troubled over the matter for whatever reasons.

Second, the issue has implications regarding both the church's ecclesiastical integrity and its spiritual unity. The troublesome issue of wine drinking has been and continues to be a source of strife and contention within Christian circles. However, rather than tolerating divisions of this sort (cf. 1 Cor. 1:11; 3:1–3), Christians are called to unity in the Spirit (1 Cor. 12:12–14; Eph. 4). But this unity of faith and practice must be based upon a sure foundation of truth, i.e., the Word of God (John 17:17; Eph. 4:14–15). Consequently, it is incumbent upon the members and leaders of a church to promote a truth-based unity on this and all other issues.

Third, the issue has implications regarding both the church's social outreach and its cultural influence. Christians are called upon to be "the light of the world" (Matt. 5:14–16) in order to expose the "deeds of darkness" (Eph. 5:11). To give proper and consistent guidance to the world regarding alcohol use will require that Christians have their biblical facts straight. We can demand neither more nor less than God's law allows.

The present study will be aimed at the exploration of what the writer deems to be the two fundamental questions involved in the whole discussion. What is the express teaching of Scripture on the use of alcoholic beverages (chapter two)? What role does the doctrine of Christian liberty play in the proper application of the Christian view of alcohol (chapter three)? In a real sense, chapter two will especially expose the error of the prohibitionist position, while chapter three will demonstrate the error of the abstentionist view.

It should not be assumed, however, that the two primary and leading questions treated herein exhaust the material of Christian ethics relevant to the alcohol question. Among other important (though secondary) matters worthy of consideration are:

1. The theological implications of each of the three positions. Given the fact that the theology of Scripture is a "seamless garment," the teachings of Scripture regarding creation, Christ,

salvation, and other doctrines are drawn into the discussion by necessary implication.[6]

2. The internal logical consistency of each position in terms of potential logical fallacies resulting from the manner of argument.[7]

3. The medical data illustrative of the effects of each position—for instance, whether alcohol might be prescribed for some persons while forbidden to others.[8]

It should be noted as well that demographic studies and sociological statistics are often helpful for putting the matter in contemporary perspective. The omission of such statistics and general knowledge from the present work is due primarily to their ready access elsewhere.[9] They are also of secondary importance to the heart issue of ethical concern: What saith the Scripture?

The Bible and Christian Ethics

Let us now turn to a scriptural analysis of the problem of the Christian, the Bible, and alcohol.

The starting point for developing a truly Christian ethical system must be the study of Scripture itself. The Christian is persuaded that God's holy will is the perfect standard of righteousness. And the Christian is further assured that God's holy will is infallibly and unchangeably revealed in the Bible. Consequently, the Bible—and the Bible *alone*—must be the starting point and supreme standard for defining truly Christian ethical behavior.

6. Cf. the writings of Cornelius Van Til for this important truth. For an introduction to the "interdependence of biblical doctrines" from a Van Til perspective, see: John M. Frame "The Problem of Theological Paradox" in Gary North, ed., *Foundations of Christian Scholarship* (Vallecito, CA: Ross House Books, 1976), pp. 295–332.

7. For a brief sample of the problem, see page 28 *infra*.

8. Robert O'Brien and Morris Chafetz, M.D., *The Encyclopedia of Alcoholism* (New York: Facts on File, 1982).

9. Cf. *Third Special Report to the U. S. Congress on Alcohol and Health from the Secretary of Health, Education, and Welfare* (Rockville, MD: National Institute on Alcohol Abuse and Alcoholism, June, 1978). Also see Nada J. Estes and Me. Edith Heinemann, *Alcoholism: Development, Consequences, and Interventions*, 2nd. ed. (St. Louis: The C. V. Mosby Co., 1982).

Reformed Christendom has beautifully distilled this truth of the preeminency of Scripture as the standard for faith and life in the Westminster Confession of Faith:

> . . . it pleased the Lord, at sundry times and in divers manners, to reveal Himself, and to declare that his will unto his church; and afterwards, for the better preserving and propagating of the truth, and for the more sure establishment and comfort of the Church against the corruption of the flesh, and the malice of Satan and of the world, to commit the same wholly unto writing: which maketh the holy Scripture to be most necessary; those former ways of God's revealing his will unto his people being now ceased[I:1].

The Scripture is God's revealed and permanent will for man. Conservative Christian thought insists upon two important ethical principles: (1) the ubiquity of ethics (i.e., the teaching that everything a man does has moral implications); and (2) the sufficiency of Scripture (i.e., the teaching that although every possible act of man is not specifically detailed in Scripture, totally sufficient principles are nevertheless revealed to adequately govern every contingency). Again we would do well to note the emphatic and pointed declaration of the Westminster Confession of Faith in this regard:

> The whole counsel of God concerning all things necessary for his own glory, man's salvation, faith and life, is either expressly set down in Scripture, or by good and necessary consequence may be deduced from Scripture: unto which nothing at any time is to be added, whether by new revelations of the Spirit, or traditions of men[I:6].

Thus it can be boldly asserted that

> The supreme judge by which all controversies of religion are to be determined, and all decrees of councils, opinions of ancient writers, doctrines of men, and private spirits, are to be determined, and in whose sentence we are to rest, can be no other but the Holy Spirit speaking in the Scripture[I:10].

These doctrinal affirmations themselves are formulated from the express teaching of Scripture: "All Scripture is inspired by God and profitable for teaching, for reproof, for correction, for training in righteousness, that the man of God may be adequate, equipped for every good work" (2 Tim. 3:16–17). To the apostles—who were divinely commissioned and supernaturally gifted bearers of the revelation of God—the Lord Jesus Christ promised, "But when He, the Spirit of truth, comes, He will guide you into all the truth . . ." (John 16:13). God's Word is unequivocal truth (John 17:17), just as Jesus Christ is the personification of God's Word (John 1:1) and truth (John 14:6). Therefore, we are under divine obligation to bring "every thought captive to the obedience of Christ" (2 Cor. 10:5). That is, we must submit *every* area of life to Christ and his will as revealed in Scripture.

In the current intellectual and spiritual climate of our times, there are numerous examples of deviation from the norm of Scripture. For example, perhaps the key heresy of Mormonism is its belief in an open canon which allows for continued "revelation" from God (*The Book of Mormon, The Doctrine and Covenants, The Pearl of Great Price,* and so on). Similarly, the ever-present danger in Pentecostalism and the charismatic movement lies in their frequent claims to continuing direct access to the mind of God through supernatural and miraculous revelatory gifts of the Holy Spirit (such as prophetic utterances, visions, glossalalia). Finally, the clear apostasy of neo-orthodoxy is its denial of propositional truth in favor of existential subjectivism (dynamic revelation, confrontational crises, and so on). These widely divergent camps suffer from a common malady: subjectivism in determining the will of God.

Unfortunately, even conservative fundamentalism often borders on this error in its ethical reliance upon "the leading of the Holy Spirit" divorced from the Word of God—sign seeking, special guidance by direct feelings and impressions of the Holy Spirit, and the like. This error is particularly relevant to the issue at hand in that it often appears to be so devout and "bib-

lical." There is a great temptation to resort to "sanctified feelings" or "common sense" in regard to complex ethical issues,
especially in our day of instant-this and freeze-dried-that.

Before entering into a survey of the biblical data that are
directly relevant to the alcohol issue, it would serve us well to
pause in reflection upon a warning issued by conservative theologian John Murray. The following paragraphs are taken from
an article by Murray entitled "The Guidance of the Holy Spirit."

The basic premise upon which we must proceed is that the
Word of God in the Scriptures of the Old and New Testaments
is the only infallible rule of practice, as it is also the only infallible
rule of faith. Complementary to this basic premise is another,
namely, that the Word of God is a perfect and sufficient rule of
practice. The corollary of this is that we may not look for, depend
upon, or demand new revelations of the Spirit. . . .

[However], we may still fall into the error of thinking that
while the Holy Spirit does not provide us with special revelations
in the form of words or visions or dreams, yet he may and does
provide us with some *direct* feeling or impression or conviction
which we may regard as the Holy Spirit's intimation to us of
what his mind and will is in a particular situation. The present
writer maintains that this view of the Holy Spirit's guidance
amounts, in effect, to the same thing as to believe that the Holy
Spirit gives special revelation. And the reason for this conclusion
is that we are, in such an event, conceiving of the Holy Spirit
as giving us some special and direct communication, be it in the
form of feeling, impression, or conviction, a communication or
intimation or direction that is not mediated to us through those
means which God has ordained for our direction and guidance.
In the final analysis this construction or conception of the Holy
Spirit's guidance is in the same category as that which holds to
direct and special revelation, and that for the reason that it
makes little difference whether the intimation is in the form of
impression or feeling or conviction or in the form of a verbal
communication, if we believe that the experience which we have
is a direct and special intimation to us of what the will of God
is. . . . We are abstracting the operation of the Spirit, in respect

of guidance, from the various factors which may properly be regarded as the means through which we are to be guided.[10]

What the world needs most today, second only to regeneration itself, is a coherent, biblically derived ethical system by which to judge all thought and behavior. Autonomous ethics are internally contradictory and inherently evil. Christian ethics must be built up from the self-authenticating Word of the Living God—not the traditions of men, whether "secular" or "religious" (cf. Matt. 15:3, 6; Mark 7:13). The resolute strength of a truly vital Christianity is its sole reliance upon all-sufficient Scripture for all matters concerning faith and practice. The inspired, infallible, inerrant Word of God is and must always be the regulative principle of Christian thought and conduct. Theologian R. B. Kuiper has well stated this precept: "All Christian teachings, whether doctrinal or ethical, are drawn from the Bible. According to Christianity the acid test of truth and goodness is Scripturalness."[11]

With this in mind, the particular problem of the Christian and alcoholic beverages can now be approached. Since material of the Christian position must be the material of Scripture, the question then must be, as stated previously: What does the Scripture teach about the consumption of alcoholic beverages?

---

10. John Murray, "The Guidance of the Holy Spirit" in *Collected Writings of John Murray*, vol. 1 (Edinburgh: The Banner of Truth Trust, 1976), pp. 186–187.

11. R. B. Kuiper, *The Bible Tells Us So* (Edinburgh: The Banner of Truth Trust, 1968), p. 17.

2

Bible Teaching on Alcoholic Beverages

The Bible and Alcohol Abuse

It should go without saying that in terms of the perspective of Scripture, drunkenness is a sinful state that merits God's disapprobation. This stance is held by the proponents of each of the three positions on alcohol. The Scripture frequently condemns drunkenness unsparingly and from a variety of considerations. Eight different scriptural angles of condemnation will be surveyed to lay before the reader the Bible's position on alcohol abuse.

1. Drunkenness is expressly condemned in Scripture. Scattered throughout the Bible are such statements as the following:

"And do not get drunk with wine . . ." (Eph. 5:18).

"Let us behave properly as in the day, not in carousing and drunkenness . . ." (Rom. 13:13).

"Now the deeds of the flesh are evident, which are: immorality, impurity, sensuality . . . envyings, drunkenness, carousings, and things like these, of which I forewarn you just as I have forewarned you that those who practice such things shall not inherit the kingdom of God" (Gal. 5:19, 21).

"But actually, I wrote to you not to associate with any so-called brother if he should be an immoral person, or covetous, or an idolater, or a reviler, or a drunkard, or a swindler—not even to eat with such a one" (1 Cor. 5:11).

"[Neither] thieves, nor the covetous, nor drunkards . . . shall inherit the kingdom of God" (1 Cor. 6:10).

The Christian, therefore, must avoid even fellowshiping with the drunkard and gluttonous:

> Do not be with heavy drinkers of wine,
> Or with gluttonous eaters of meat (Prov. 23:20).

2. Drunkenness is a curse on man. Not only is drunkenness forbidden by direct prohibition, but its presence in a society is an aspect of the very curse of God.

"Thus says the LORD, 'Behold, I am about to fill all the inhabitants of this land . . . with drunkenness! And I will dash them against each other . . . [and] destroy them' " (Jer. 13:13–14).

> For thus says the Lord GOD, "Behold, I will give you into the hand of those whom you hate, into the hand of those from whom you were alienated. . . .
>
> You will be filled with drunkenness and sorrow,
> The cup of horror and desolation . . ." (Ezek. 23:28, 33).

Thus, drunkenness inevitably leads to ruin and destruction, the very opposite condition of the blessing of God:

> For the heavy drinker and the glutton will come to poverty,
> And drowsiness will clothe a man with rags (Prov. 23:21).
>
> Whatever you devise against the LORD,
> He will make a complete end of it.
> Distress will not rise up twice.
> Like tangled thorns,
> And like those who are drunken with their drink,
> They are consumed
> As stubble completely withered (Nah. 1:9–10).
>
> Woe to you who make your neighbors drink,
> Who mix in your venom even to make them drunk
> So as to look on their nakedness!

You will be filled with disgrace rather than honor.
Now you yourself drink and expose your own nakedness.
The cup in the LORD'S right hand will come around to you,
And utter disgrace will come upon your glory (Hab. 2:15–16).

Rejoice and be glad, O daughter of Edom,
Who dwells in the land of Uz;
But the cup will come around to you as well,
You will become drunk and make yourself naked.
The punishment of your iniquity has been completed, O daughter
    of Zion;
He will exile you no longer.
But He will punish your iniquity, O daughter of Edom;
He will expose your sins! (Lam. 4:21–22).

3. Drunkenness distorts one's perception of God's world. In Scripture it will be seen that drunkenness causes an illusory detachment from the real world that God has created:

Who has woe? Who has sorrow?
Who has contentions? Who has complaining?
Who has wounds without cause?
Who has redness of eyes? Those who linger long over wine,
Those who go to taste mixed wine. . . .
Your eyes will see strange things,
And your mind will utter perverse things (Prov. 23:29–30, 33).

And they shall drink and stagger and go mad because of the sword that I will send among them (Jer. 25:16).

. . . They are confused by wine, they stagger by strong drink;
They reel while having visions . . . (Isa. 28:7).

These passages explain why some in great sorrow and others who are miserable failures often pursue drink to the point of drunkenness. Alcohol serves as an escape mechanism that releases them from the burdens of the reality of their condition: "Harlotry, wine, and new wine take away the understanding" (Hos. 4:11).

This, of course, is ultimately counterproductive, bringing more heaviness of heart: "[Jesus said:] Be on guard, that your hearts may not be weighted down with dissipation and drunkenness and the worries of life . . ." (Luke 21:34).

4. Drunkenness destroys one's vocational capacity. One of the biblical directives regulative of the office of king (and, by extension, to any vocation to civil government) is found in Proverbs. There it is noted that while engaging in the affairs of state, kings are forbidden indulgence in wine:

> It is not for kings, O Lemuel,
> It is not for kings to drink wine,
> Or for rulers to desire strong drink (Prov. 31:4).

The rationale behind this directive is immediately appended:

> Lest they drink and forget what is decreed,
> And pervert the rights of the afflicted (v. 5).

This same idea appears in a similar context, where Isaiah sarcastically prophesies: "Woe to those who are heroes in drinking wine, and valiant men in mixing strong drink; who justify the wicked for a bribe, and take away the rights of the ones who are in the right!" (Isa. 5:22–23; cf. 28:6–7).

Wine has the capacity to dull one's ratiocinative abilities and thus has the potential for destroying one's vocational function when indulged in immoderately. And this predicament is not limited to the political realm. The decline of one's productive output in any vocation is set forth in proverb by Solomon: "Do not be with heavy drinkers of wine, or with gluttonous eaters of meat; for the heavy drinker and the glutton will come to poverty, and drowsiness will clothe a man with rags" (Prov. 23:20–21).

5. Drunkenness is socially disgusting. Drunkenness leads men to behavior widely at variance with godly and orderly expectations:

"And these also reel with wine and stagger from strong drink; . . . For all the tables are full of filthy vomit, without a single clean place" (Isa. 28:7–8).

". . . Thus says the LORD of hosts, the God of Israel, 'Drink, be drunk, vomit, fall, and rise no more . . ." (Jer. 25:27). "They reeled and staggered like a drunken man . . ." (Ps. 107:27).

They grope in darkness with no light
And He makes them stagger like a drunken man (Job 12:25).

Not only is the conduct of the drunkard disorderly and repulsive, but he also becomes possessed of a contentious spirit that makes him socially obnoxious:

Wine is a mocker, strong drink a brawler,
And whoever is intoxicated by it is not wise (Prov. 20:1).

Here, by process of metonymy,[1] the wine is substituted for the drunkard himself (who is so closely associated with the wine). That is, it is actually the drunkard who is the "mocker" and "brawler." Proverbs 23 also makes reference to the contentious spirit generated by drunkenness:

Who has woe? Who has sorrow?
Who has contentions? . . .
Those who linger long over wine . . . (Prov. 23:29–30).

6. Drunkenness weakens the body. The body of man is the handiwork of God (Gen. 2:7) and as such should inspire our awe of God's marvelous creative power and glorious wisdom (Ps. 139:13–15; Job 10:8–12; Eccles. 11:5). As Christians it is incumbent upon us to maintain the health of our bodies, for the body is the temple of the Holy Spirit (1 Cor. 3:16–17; 6:19–20; 2 Cor. 6:16). But to "linger long at the wine" is physically dan-

---

1. A *metonymy* is a figure of speech that "means using the name of one thing for another thing because the two are frequently associated together or because the one may suggest the other. A common example of metonymy is the use of 'the White House' to refer to the President, e.g. 'The White House decided to release the speech earlier than usual.' " Cited from A. Berkley Mickelsen, *Interpreting the Bible* (Grand Rapids: Eerdmans, 1963), pp. 185–186.

gerous because at the last "it bites like a serpent" and "stings like a viper" (Prov. 23:30, 32).

Thus, overindulgence can lead one to become "sick with the heat of wine" (Hos. 7:5a). Indeed, it is the case that "a drunken man staggers in his vomit" (Isa. 19:14c).

Although our concern in this book is to get at the biblical data on alcohol abuse, it should be kept in mind that it is a medically proven fact that overindulgence in alcohol can result in serious debilitating harm to the alcoholic.[2] Thus, chronic alcoholism (as both Scripture and experience teach) is destructive of physical well-being. In contrast to such dangers resident in alcohol abuse, Christians are under divine obligation to nourish and cherish their bodies (Eph. 5:29). God is concerned with our good health. As a matter of fact, many of the case laws of the Old Testament were health and sanitation dictums designed to foster bodily strength.[3]

7. Drunkenness corrupts morals. Moral sensitivity is greatly diminished when the mind is overcome by excessive alcohol intake. The classic illustration of this phenomenon, of course, is history's first recorded episode of drunkenness in the case of Noah: "And he drank of the wine and became drunk, and uncovered himself inside his tent" (Gen. 9:21).

In another verse the daughters of Lot connived to wash away their father's moral restraints by use of wine: "Come, let us make our father drink wine, and let us lie with him, that we may preserve our family through our father" (Gen. 19:32). Their evil plan was successful (vv. 33–38).

2. Although medically it seems to be true that alcohol itself "does not cause any known damage to the body" (Morris E. Chafetz, M.D., *Liquor: The Servant of Man* [Toronto: Little, Brown and Company, 1965], p. 65), nevertheless, the manner and the quantities in which it is consumed can and do indirectly cause various ailments. For instance, the vomiting associated with *excessive* consumption can lead to esophagitis due to the increased acid production by the stomach and frequent agitation of the esophogal lining by vomiting action. For additional medical research on the effects of chronic alcoholism see: O'Brien, *Encyclopedia, passim* (note 8, chapter one) and Estes, *Alcoholism* (note 9, chapter one), chs. 7–13.

3. E.g., R. J. Rushdoony, *Institutes of Biblical Law*, vol. 1 (Nutley, NJ: Craig, 1973), pp. 293–301.

Such potential immorality among the drunken later becomes material for prophetic curse: ". . . You will become drunk and make yourself naked" (Lam. 4:21); "They have also cast lots for My people, / Traded a boy for a harlot, / And sold a girl for wine that they may drink" (Joel 3:3). Consequently, it is not surprising that overindulgence in wine causes spiritual indifference, as illustrated in Isaiah 5:11–12:

> Woe to those who rise early in the morning that they may pursue
>   strong drink;
> Who stay up late in the evening that wine may inflame them!
> And their banquets are accompanied by lyre and harp, by tam-
>   bourine and flute, and by wine;
> But they do not pay attention to the deeds of the LORD,
> Nor do they consider the work of His hands.

Thus, too, drunkenness is frequently included in verses relating a complex of immoral vices inimical to Christian conduct (Rom. 13:13; Gal. 5:19–21; 1 Peter 4:3–4).

8. Drunkenness bars one from church leadership. Paul mentions this several times in his pastoral letters when he outlines the prerequisites for both ordained ecclesiastical office and other forms of church service:

"An overseer [i.e., elder], then, must be . . . not addicted to wine . . ." (1 Tim. 3:2–3); and "Deacons likewise must be men of dignity, not double-tongued, or addicted to much wine . . ." (v. 8). Similarly, "Older women likewise are to be reverent in their behavior, not malicious gossips, not enslaved to much wine . . ." (Titus 2:3).

This restriction is made not only because drunkenness is itself a heinous sin (points 1, 2, and 7 above)—not only due to the necessity of a church leader's being possessed of clarity of thought and facility of mind in order to properly "think God's thoughts after Him" (points 3, 4, and 6 above)—but also because the leader is to be an example to the church (Heb. 13:17) and to the world (1 Tim. 3:7; 2 Tim. 2:24–26), living a life of godliness (contra points 5 and 7 above).

The biblical data is crystal clear relative to the issue of all forms of alcohol abuse (whether occasional indulgence, binge drunkenness, or chronic alcoholism). With unmistakable emphasis the Scripture condemns drunkenness on physiological and social grounds as well as for spiritual and moral reasons. God's manifest disapprobation is toward those who "linger long at the wine" and are "given to much wine."

However, having noted these important matters, one must be careful to avoid wrongly equating drunkenness with drinking. To condemn *all* use of alcoholic beverage—whether occasional, moderate, sacramental, or medicinal—by resorting to scriptural prohibitions against *drunkenness* would be to engage in fallacious ethical reasoning. Perhaps the error of such reasoning can best be illustrated syllogistically, as follows:

1. Scripture condemns drunkenness.	1. Scripture condemns gluttony.	1. Scripture condemns sexual perversion.
2. Drinking can lead to drunkenness.	2. Eating can lead to gluttony.	2. Enjoyment of sex can lead to sexual perversion.
3. Therefore: Scripture condemns all drinking.	3. Therefore: Scripture condemns all eating.	3. Therefore: Scripture condemns all sexual enjoyment.

Looking at the matter in this way, it is obvious that just because Scripture condemns drunkenness (an *abuse* of alcohol), it does not necessarily follow that it also condemns moderate, occasional, and temperate drinking of alcoholic beverages (a *use* of alcohol). Although gluttony is at times paralleled in Scripture with drunkenness (Deut. 21:20; Prov. 23:21), surely *all* eating is not condemned! Sexual perversion is also paralleled in Scripture with drunkenness (Rom. 13:13; 1 Peter 4:3), but who would condemn *all* sexual activity?

It is obvious that our investigation of the matter of the Christian, the Bible, and alcohol must continue further.

The Old Testament and Alcohol Use

To properly understand the scriptural pronouncements on alcohol consumption, it will be necessary to engage in a lexical analysis of the various Hebrew and Greek words that are most prominently employed of alcoholic drink in Scripture. Although there are numerous Hebrew terms employed in the Old Testament, the present study will concentrate on four particularly significant words: *yayin*, *shekar*, *tirosh*, and *'asis*. (In the New Testament, two Greek words will require our attention: *oinos* and *gleukos*.)

yayin

The most common word for wine in the Old Testament is *yayin*, which occurs in the Hebrew text 141 times. It is apparently a word borrowed from another language, and its root meaning is somewhat obscure.[4] However, it is widely recognized as being functionally equivalent to the Greek term *oinos* and the Latin *vinum*.[5]

J. D. Davis has pointed out that *yayin* must be seen to be an intoxicant based on the interpretive principle of "first mention," as well as extensive inductive research of the Scriptures: "When the Hebrew word *yayin* first occurs in Scripture, it is the fermented juice of the grape (Gen. 9:21), and there is no reason to believe that it has a different meaning elsewhere."[6]

Even fundamentalist Old Testament scholar Merrill F. Unger has observed:

> In most of the passages in the Bible where *yayin* is used . . . it certainly means *fermented grape juice*, and in the remainder it may be fairly presumed to do so. . . . In no passage can it be

4. Brown-Driver-Briggs, p. 406.

5. E.g., *ibid.*, p. 406. See also Burton Scott Easton, "Wine," *ISBE*, IV:3086; Dunlop Moore, "Wine," in Philip Schaff, ed., *A Religious Encyclopedia of Biblical, Historical, Doctrinal and Practical Theology* (Chicago: Funk and Wagnalls, 1887), III:2536; John D. Davis, "Wine," in *Illustrated Davis Bible Dictionary* (Nashville: Royal Publishers, 1973 rep), p. 867.

6. Davis, *Dictionary*, p. 867.

positively shown to have any other meaning. The intoxicating character of *yayin* in general is plain from Scripture.[7]

Those who insist that intoxication was not within the capacity of *yayin* are quite mistaken and are set against well-established lexical authorities. And those who attempt to argue that there were two types of *yayin*—one fermented and the other unfermented—fare no better. For instance, Stephen M. Reynolds, a translator of the New International Version and an able proponent of mandatory total abstinence, has argued:

> *Yayin* is assumed by many people to be always an alcoholic drink. This is a mistake which has led to much confusion and to much intoxication which might easily have been avoided. Isaiah 16:10 says: "No treader shall tread out *yayin* in the presses." This obviously means that no treader shall tread out grape juice in the presses, because fermentation is a time consuming process. Therefore alcohol is excluded from the word *yayin* in this passage.[8]

He then immediately adds: "This is enough to establish the fact that *yayin* in the Bible need not be alcoholic."[9]

However, despite the *prima facie* plausibility of this argument, a closer consideration of Isaiah 16:10 demonstrates that Reynolds's point lacks sufficient merit. Indeed, his argument is not only exegetically confused but logically inconsistent with other statements and principles contained within his own book. Exegetically it should be noted that the verse in question is lifted from a poetic context. And the poetic imagery so common in Hebrew poetry will allow *yayin* here to be alcoholic. Two examples will be brought forward by way of illustration. Both of these examples are especially relevant in that they involve the notion of time, which is vital to the Reynolds argument.

In the third chapter of Job, the downcast Job begins his poetic lamentation of his woeful circumstances. There he curses both the night of his conception and the day of his birth. The specifics

---

7. Merrill F. Unger, *Unger's Bible Dictionary* (Chicago: Moody Press, 1970 ed.), p. 1168.

8. Reynolds, p. 20.

9. *Ibid.*

of his anguished song are most interesting: "Let the day perish on which I was to be born, and the night which said, 'A boy is conceived' " (Job 3:3). A consultation of the Hebrew text reveals that what is said to have been conceived was a *geber*. According to the Brown-Driver-Briggs *Lexicon*, this term means "man."[10] As a matter of fact, it goes on to show that the term speaks not simply of maleness, but "man as strong, disting(uished) fr(om) women, children and non-combatants whom he is to defend."[11] Yet Job employed accepted poetic license to call his own just-conceived zygote a "man," as if he were at that moment a mature adult man. Likewise, Isaiah used *yayin* to refer to the freshly expressed juice of the grape as if it were at that moment aged, or fermented.

In Job 10 is found a somewhat similar situation. In verse 10 Job speaks of his father's semen, from which he would eventually arise (i.e., after the union of sperm and ovum), as "me." As I have argued elsewhere,[12] human personhood *does* begin at the very moment of conception. Thus it is quite appropriate to use the personal pronoun "me" when speaking of the fertilized ovum (*conceptus*). However, this is not *literally* accurate when making reference to the semen itself: semen is not a person. Yet, according to such noted exegetes as Franz Delitzsch,[13] S. R. Driver, G. B. Gray,[14] and others, this is exactly what Job was referring to by his reference to "milk" in Job 10:10a: "Didst Thou not pour me out like milk?" Again, poetic license allows such an *effecta pro causa*, i.e., it allows the eventual end product to stand for the seed-beginning. In Job "me" is applied to semen, while in Isaiah *yayin* (fermented wine) is applied to freshly expressed grape juice. In both cases the mature, end product was in mind.

10. Brown-Driver-Briggs, p. 150.

11. *Ibid.*, p. 150.

12. See my *The Christian Case Against Abortion* (Mauldin, SC: GoodBirth, 1982), pp. 12–28.

13. Franz Delitzsch, *Job*, volume 1, in C. F. Keil and Franz Delitzsch, *Commentary on the Old Testament* (Grand Rapids: Eerdmans, rep. 1975), p. 167.

14. S. R. Driver and G. B. Gray, *A Critical and Exegetical Commentary on the Book of Job* in *The International Critical Commentary* (Edinburgh: T & T Clark, rep. 1977), p. 100.

Clearly then, Reynolds has erred in arguing as he did from Isaiah 16:10. The error is serious enough in that he emphasized it as "enough to establish the fact" (which it does not). But then he employs it again later in subsequent argumentation as an assured observation (cf. Reynolds, p. 28). The error becomes totally inexcusable when later in the same book he makes observations that in principle totally overthrow his own case.

For instance, on page 25 of his book, Reynolds makes reference to *tirosh*, which is another word for "wine," or—given his argument—"grape juice." There he notes that "reference to its being found in the cluster (Isa. 65:8) and to its suffering in time of drought (Isa. 24:7) are understood to be poetical."[15] Precisely! Just as *tirosh* can be said to be found in "cluster" (Isa. 65:8), so can *yayin* (fermented wine) be said to be "treaded out from grapes" (Isa. 16:10).

To compound his error Reynolds argues by a very similar method (proleptic statement) in regard to Ephesians 5:18:

> Some commentators say that the words "in which" refer to the whole phrase, "Be not drunk with wine," and not just to "wine." The wish not to accept the idea that debauchery is "in" wine makes them reject this obvious sense, and choose instead the idea that it lies in being drunk. *But end results are sometimes attributed to the substance which causes the results.*[16]

It should be obvious to the careful reader that this principle of "end results," if legitimate in the prose of Ephesians 5,[17] should be equally legitimate in the poetry of Isaiah 16:10. That is, based on Reynolds's own argument, *yayin* (fermented juice) *could* be said to be "treaded out in the presses" in that "end results are sometimes attributed to the substance which causes the result."[18] The critical argument put forward by Reynolds is not established at all.

15. Reynolds, p. 25.
16. *Ibid.*, p. 53. Emphasis mine.
17. However, the present writer does not agree that this was Paul's intention; see my later discussion on p. 47 *infra*.
18. *Ibid.*, p. 53.

Dunlop Moore provides us with a studied comment on the matter at hand when he writes:

> The references to wine-making in the Bible let us see that no effort was made to preserve the expressed juice of the grape from exposure to the air; and it would, of course, ferment. But long before it was matured, so as to be proper *yayin*, it could intoxicate: hence we find an inebriating power ascribed to *'asis* (Isa. 49:26) and to *tirosh* (Hos. 4:11), and to *gleukos* (Acts 2:13). . . . In fact, the theory of two kinds of wine—the one fermented and intoxicating and unlawful, and the other unfermented, unintoxicating, and lawful—is a modern hypothesis, devised during the present century, and has no foundation in the Bible, or in Hebrew or classical antiquity.[19]

Likewise, C. M. Kerr, writing in the classic *International Standard Bible Encyclopedia*, states categorically that "To insist on a distinction between intoxicating and unfermented wine is a case of unjustified special pleading."[20] Unger agrees: "Some, indeed, have argued from these passages [i.e., passages speaking favorably of *yayin*] that *yayin* could not always have been alcoholic. But this is begging the question, and that in defiance of the facts."[21]

That *yayin* possessed the potential to inebriate is evident in the cases of Noah (Gen. 9:21), Lot (Gen. 19:32–35), and Nabal (1 Sam. 25:37), to name but a few. These men are examples of men who became tragically drunk and morally degraded by abusive employment of *yayin.* Yet, at the same time, it is also used in a number of righteous ways.

1. *Yayin* is given as a gift between godly men. Melchizedek, who was a "priest of God Most High" (Gen. 14:18) and at the very least a type of Christ (Ps. 110:4; Heb. 5:6, 10; 6:20)—and who *may* have even been a theophanic manifestation of Christ[22]—gave *yayin* to faithful Abraham in Genesis 14:18–20:

19. Moore, *Encyclopedia*, III:2536–2537.

20. C. M. Kerr, "Drunkenness," in *ISBE*, II:881.

21. Unger, *Dictionary*, p. 1168.

22. See discussions of this issue in: Philip E. Hughes, *A Commentary on the Epistle to the Hebrews* (Grand Rapids: Eerdmans, 1977), pp. 237ff. A. W. Pink, *An Exposition of Hebrews* (Grand Rapids: Baker, 1954), pp. 360ff.); F. W. Schultz, "Melchizedek," in Philip Schaff, ed., *A Religious Encyclopedia*, II:1462ff; Charles H. Spurgeon, *The Treasury of David* (New York: Funk and Wagnalls, 1881), V:202.

And Melchizedek king of Salem brought out bread and wine;
now he was a priest of God Most High. And he blessed him and
said, "Blessed be Abram of God Most High, Possessor of heaven
and earth; And blessed be God Most High, who has delivered
your enemies into your hand." And he gave him a tenth of all.

This was done in the very context of God's blessing and without
the least inkling of disapprobation.

2. *Yayin* is commanded to be brought as an offering to God.
This practice is frequently alluded to in the law of God: "Now
this is what you shall offer on the altar: . . . one-tenth of an
ephah of fine flour mixed with one-fourth of a hin of beaten oil,
and one-fourth of a hin of wine for a libation with one lamb"
(Exod. 29:38, 40). "Its grain offering shall then be two-tenths
of an ephah of fine flour mixed with oil, an offering by fire to
the LORD for a soothing aroma, with its libation, a fourth of a
hin of wine" (Lev. 23:13). "And you shall prepare wine for the
libation, one-fourth of a hin, with the burnt offering or for the
sacrifice, for each lamb. . . . and for the libation you shall offer
one-third of a hin of wine as a soothing aroma to the LORD.
. . . and you shall offer as the libation one-half a hin of wine as
an offering by fire, as a soothing aroma to the LORD" (Num.
15:5, 7, 10).

This factor has a double significance for the present discussion. On the one hand, if wine were considered to be evil, the
question arises as to why God would require wine as an offering
to himself. On the other hand, if it were commanded as an
offering, it is obvious that the people of God in the Old Testament were required to produce it—at least for sacrificial purposes!

3. *Yayin* is considered by inspired writers of Scripture to be
a gracious blessing of God. If the Israelites faithfully differen-
tiated between clean and unclean animals (Deut. 14:3–21),
tithed (v. 22), and lived obediently before God (v. 23), then
God promised them that they "may spend the money for whatever your heart desires, for oxen, or sheep, or wine, or strong
drink, or whatever your heart desires; and there you shall eat in

the presence of the LORD your God and rejoice, you and your household" (v. 26).

Psalm 104:14–15 reads that God

> causes the grass to grow for the cattle,
>   And vegetation for the labor of man,
>   So that he may bring forth food from the earth,
> And wine which makes man's heart glad,
>   So that he may make his face glisten with oil,
>   And food which sustains man's heart.

Interestingly, here food and wine and oil are joined together as a blessing; whereas in Proverbs 23:20–21 food and wine—when overindulged in—serve as a curse. Again, *use* must be distinguished from *abuse*. A moderate "gladdening of the heart" was not forbidden, according to this and other Scriptures (cf. 2 Sam. 13:28; Esther 1:10; Eccles. 9:7; 10:19; Zech. 9:15; 10:7).

In Ecclesiastes 9 Solomon expounds the theme that men are in the almighty hand of God. In verse 7 he exhorts men to "Go then, eat your bread in happiness, and drink your wine with a cheerful heart; for God has already approved your works." In Isaiah 55:1 God's free offer of mercy is likened to the free reception of water, wine, and milk:

> Ho! Every one who thirsts, come to the waters;
> And you who have no money come, buy and eat.
> Come, buy wine and milk
> Without money and without cost.

Thus, *yayin* by extension can serve as a fitting symbol of the glad blessings (cf. Ps. 104:14–15) of the prophesied messianic era. In Amos 9:13–15 we read:

> "Behold, days are coming," declares the LORD,
> "When the plowman will overtake the reaper,
> And the treader of grapes him who sows seed;
> When the mountains will drip sweet wine,
> And all the hills will be dissolved.

> Also I will restore the captivity of My people Israel
> And they will rebuild the ruined cities and live in them;
> They will also plant vineyards and drink their wine
> And make gardens and eat their fruit.
> I will also plant them on their land,
> And they will not again be rooted out from their land
> Which I have given them,"
> Says the LORD your God.

Isaiah puts the matter this way:

> And the LORD of hosts will prepare a lavish banquet for all
>   peoples on this mountain;
> A banquet of aged wine, choice pieces with marrow,
> And refined, aged wine (Isa. 25:6).

4. *Yayin* is removed from Israel as an expression of divine curse. Deuteronomy 28 is a most significant chapter dealing with God's covenant with Israel (and with *any* community or culture). The first fourteen verses outline concrete covenantal blessings to be granted to Israel if they are obedient. Verses 15 through 68 outline concrete aspects of God's curse consequent upon Israel's disobedience to God. For the present study, verse 39 is most instructive: "You shall plant and cultivate vineyards, but you shall neither drink of the wine nor gather the grapes, for the worm shall devour them." God's curse would remove *all* good things from the disobedient culture: farm animals (v. 31), covenant children (vv. 32, 41), agricultural produce (vv. 33, 38, 42), olive trees (v. 40), grape vines and wine (v. 39), and so forth.

Having surveyed various commendations of *yayin*, it should be noted before moving on to other matters, that *yayin* can be employed metaphorically in a bad sense. Just as leaven can be symbolic of evil's penetrating, corrupting power (cf. Matt. 16:6; 1 Cor. 5:8), so wine can serve as a metaphor of something disastrous: the wrath of God against his enemies, as in Psalm 60:5, 7; 78:65; and Jeremiah 25:15. Yet, also like leaven (cf. Lev. 7:13; 23:17; Matt. 13:33), it can just as easily be emblematic of something good; wine may represent godly wisdom (Prov. 9:2–5), the joy of human love (Song of Sol. 5:1), and the gospel of God's saving grace (Isa. 55:1).

tirosh

This Hebrew word is the Old Testament's second most frequently occurring word for "wine," appearing 38 times in the Old Testament text. It properly designates the "must, fresh, or new wine."[23] It is translated by the Authorized Version (King James) most often as either "wine" or "new wine." It is derived from the Hebrew stem yarash, which means "take possession of, inherit, dispossess." Thus, as the Brown-Driver-Briggs Lexicon notes, tirosh can be either "enlivening" or "injurious."[24]

Tirosh was technically a form of immature yayin, an early stage in the fermentation process. When it is linked with "corn" (daghn) in the Old Testament, it is often so done in order to emphasize that these elements are the raw products out of which will be made the finished products of bread and wine. This is clearly evident in Genesis 27:28: "Now may God give you of the dew of heaven, And of the fatness of the earth, And an abundance of grain and new wine." On the other hand, "bread" (lechem) is found in conjunction with "wine" (yayin), as in Judges 19:19; 1 Samuel 16:20; Nehemiah 5:15, and so on. Lechem and yayin are the finished products made from daghn and tirosh.

However, this does not preclude tirosh from possessing intoxicating qualities. According to the International Standard Bible Encyclopedia:

> . . . unfermented grape juice is a very difficult thing to keep without the aid of modern antiseptic precautions, and its preservation in the warm and not overcleanly conditions of ancient Pal. was impossible. Consequently tirosh came to mean wine that was not fully aged (although with full intoxicating properties, Jds. 9:13; Hos. 4:11; cf. Acts 2:13) or wine when considered specifically as the product of grapes (Deut. 12:17; 18:4).[25]

23. Brown-Driver-Briggs, p. 440.
24. Ibid., tirosh entry at p. 1066 refers to yarash entry at p. 440. The yarash entry on p. 439 yields this definition of the root verb itself.
25. Easton, ISBE, V:3086.

Hosea 4 (alluded to in the above quotation) speaks of the moral degradation of Israel in multiplying their sins before God (v. 7). Then in verse 11 the prophet laments that "harlotry, wine, and new wine [*tirosh*] take away the understanding." That is, men are intoxicated by "new wine," as well as by "wine" (*yayin*).

But, just as with *yayin*, *tirosh* can be used righteously. In Genesis 27:28 and 37 Isaac blesses Jacob by calling on God to bless him with "abundance of grain and new wine" [*tirosh*]. It is often referred to as an explicit blessing of God as in the following Scripture passages:

> And He will love you and bless you and multiply you; He will also bless the fruit of your womb and the fruit of your ground, your grain and your new wine . . . [Deut. 7:13].

> . . .He will give the rain for your land in its season, the early and late rain, that you may gather in your grain and your new wine and your oil [Deut. 11:14].

> So your barns will be filled with plenty,
> And your vats will overflow with new wine [Prov. 3:10].

> The LORD has sworn by His right hand
>   and by His strong arm, "I will never again give your grain as
>   food for your enemies;
> Nor will foreigners drink your new wine,
>   for which you have labored" [Isa. 62:8].

> For what comeliness and beauty will be theirs!
> Grain will make the young men flourish, and new wine the virgins [Zech. 9:17].

Removal of new wine (*tirosh*) from the land is an aspect of curse (e.g., Deut. 28:51), as in the case of *yayin*.

'asis

This word occurs only five times and is translated either "sweet wine," "new wine," or "juice" in the Authorized Version. The word itself actually means "pressed out."[26] In Malachi 4:3 (Mal. 3:21 in the Hebrew text) its verb stem is used in speaking of God's "treading down" the wicked. Thus, 'asis is properly the newly expressed juice of the grape.

Yet again, despite the seeming innocence of this word lexically, 'asis can and does have the power to intoxicate. In Joel 1:5 the word of the Lord that Joel prophesied to Israel made reference to such:

> Awake, drunkards, and weep;
> And wail, all you wine drinkers,
> On account of the sweet wine ['asis]
> That is cut off from your mouth.

In Isaiah 49:26 'asis is used metaphorically in a sense that demands its inebriatory potential: "And I will feed your oppressors with their own flesh, and they will become drunk with their own blood as with sweet wine ['asis]."

However, 'asis is employed in two messianic passages as emblems of the gracious blessings of God. In Joel 3:18 we read:

> And it will come about in that day
> That the mountains will drip with sweet wine ['asis],
> And the hills will flow with milk. . . .

(Interestingly, Joel uses 'asis in both a good and a bad sense, as a comparison of this passage with the previous one in Joel 1:5 demonstrates.)

Amos 9:13 likewise promises:

> "Behold, days are coming," declares the LORD,
> "When the plowman will overtake the reaper
> And the treader of grapes him who sows seed;
> When the mountains will drip sweet wine ['asis],
> And all the hills will be dissolved."

26. Brown-Driver-Briggs, p. 779.

shekar

This word occurs 22 times in the Old Testament and literally means "intoxicating drink, strong drink."[27] It is based on the verb *shakar*, which means "to be, or become, drunk, drunken."[28] It is related to the word *shikkar* ("drunkard") and *shikkaron* ("drunkenness").[29] In the *International Standard Bible Encyclopedia* it is noted that *shekar* "appears to mean 'intoxicating drink' of any sort."[30] Furthermore, it is noted:

> With the exception of Nu. 28:7, "strong drink" is always coupled with "wine." The two terms are commonly used as mutually exclusive, and as together exhaustive of all kinds of intoxicants. . . .
>
> Thus, *shekar* is a comprehensive term for all kinds of fermented drinks [i.e., from dates, apples, barley, etc.], excluding wine.[31]

Not only is it etymologically demonstrable that *shekar* possessed the potential to inebriate, but most versions translate it in such a way as to indicate such: "strong drink" (NASB, KJV, ASV, AB), "liquor" (*Moffatt*), "hard liquor" (LB), "beer" (NIV), and so on.

But even beyond its etymological considerations and translational consensus, the Scripture itself records instances of either actual or alleged cases of drunkenness resultant from imbibing *shekar*. In 1 Samuel 1:12–15 Eli accuses Hannah of being drunk because of her unusual conduct:

> Now it came about, as she continued praying before the LORD, that Eli was watching her mouth. As for Hannah, she was speaking in her heart, only her lips were moving, but her voice was not heard. So Eli thought she was drunk. Then Eli said to her, "how long will you make yourself drunk? Put away your wine

27. *Ibid.*, p. 1016.
28. *Ibid.*
29. Kerr, *ISBE*, II:880.
30. Easton, *ISBE*, IV:3086.
31. Kerr, *ISBE*, II:879.

from you." But Hannah answered and said, "No, my lord, I am
a woman oppressed in spirit; I have drunk neither wine nor strong
drink [shekar], but I have poured out my soul before the LORD."

In the well-known Proverbs 20:1 passage, shekar is called a
"brawler" in that it has the potential to spur a troublesome,
contentious spirit in the drunkard. In Isaiah 5:11 a woe is called
down upon those who seek to be drunken with either an immoderate use of wine or strong drink: "Woe to those who rise
early in the morning that they may pursue strong drink; Who
stay up late in the evening that wine may inflame them!"

Kerr comments that in light of such passages, "the attempt
made to prove that it was simply the unfermented juice of certain
fruits is quite without foundation."[32]

Yet, shekar, rather than being prohibited and discouraged, is
commanded as a drink-offering to the Lord in Numbers 28:7:
"Then the libation with it shall be a fourth of a hin for each
lamb, in the holy place you shall pour out a libation of strong
drink [shekar] to the LORD." This is significant in that it implies
both its manufacture and production by devout Jews, and in that
it can be an offering to the Lord.

Finally we come to the locus classicus in the debate over shekar
and its tolerance in God's law: Deuteronomy 14:22–26, where
the "rejoicing tithe" is defined:

> You shall surely tithe all the produce from what you sow,
> which comes out of the field every year. And you shall eat in
> the presence of the LORD your God, at the place where He
> chooses to establish His name, the tithe of your grain, your new
> wine, your oil, and the first-born of your herd and your flock, in
> order that you may learn to fear the LORD your God always. And
> if the distance is so great for you that you are not able to bring
> the tithe . . . then you shall exchange it for money. . . . And
> you may spend the money for whatever your heart desires, for
> oxen, or sheep, or wine, or strong drink [shekar], or whatever
> your heart desires; and there you shall eat in the presence of the
> LORD your God and rejoice, you and your household.

32. Ibid., p. 880.

The thrust of this passage is unambiguous, and the divine sanction is unmistakable: *shekar* was not only allowed of God's people
but could be enjoyed "in the presence of the LORD" (v. 26) if
partaken in "the fear of God" (v. 23).[33]

In light of the wealth of evidence above, one can but incred-
ulously wonder at the following statement by Christian scholar
and scientist Henry M. Morris:

> In the Old Testament two Hebrew words ("terosh" and "yayin")
> are both translated "wine," the former meaning the fresh juice
> of the grape and the latter the fermented or decayed juice. . . .
> It is significant that nowhere does the Bible actually endorse the
> drinking of wine or other intoxicating drink.[34]

Such a statement by a prohibitionist is wholly without merit.

In conclusion, it is the case that the Old Testament considered *all* sorts of wines as blessings, even though they had the
potential for abuse and could be transformed by sinful man into
a curse. The Old Testament knows nothing of "safe" and "unsafe" wines; it is totally silent on any supposed attempt to keep
wine from undergoing natural fermentation. In Nehemiah 5,
Nehemiah is presented as a righteous servant of God, faithfully
doing the Lord's work. In verses 16 through 19 we have recorded
for us Nehemiah's humble and godly plea for God's remembrance
of *all* his conduct, a part of which was the furnishing of "all sorts
of wine in abundance":

> And I also applied myself to the work on this wall; we did not
> buy any land, and all my servants were gathered there for the

33. The best the prohibitionist can do with this passage is to divert attention away
from it by appeal to the "analogy of Scripture" as it is understood in terms of their
presuppositions. Reynolds does this on page 23 of his work: "Where it [*shekar*] is used
in Deuteronomy 14:26 it can be argued from the general consistency of all the Scripture
that it was not an intoxicant." And this despite the clear, compelling and overwhelming
exegetical, translational, and contextual considerations!

34. Henry M. Morris, *The Bible Has the Answer* (Nutley, NJ: The Craig Press,
1971), p. 162.

work. Moreover, there were at my table one hundred and fifty Jews and officials, besides those who came to us from the nations that were around us. Now that which was prepared for each day was one ox and six choice sheep, also birds were prepared for me; and once in ten days *all sorts of wines were furnished in abundance.* Yet for all this I did not demand the governor's food allowance, because the servitude was heavy on this people. Remember me, O my God, for good, according to all that I have done for this people [emphasis added].

The case for the moderationist position is so strong in the Old Testament that even the 1977 abstentionist report[35] by the "Study Committee on Beverage Use of Alcohol" of the (former) Reformed Presbyterian Church, Evangelical Synod, was compelled to admit: "The selectively specific cases of abstinence are an indicator that the Mosaic code did not make total abstinence a universally absolute rule in Israel."[36]

Abstentionist Harold Lindsell agrees when he writes:

> Since the body of the believer is the temple of the Holy Spirit, it is not difficult to conclude that abstinence is to be preferred even though *there is no express prohibition in Scripture against the use of alcohol in moderation.* [37]

Strangely, prohibitionist Stephen M. Reynolds attempts to circumvent the obvious implications of the exegetical and lexical evidence in support of the moderationist position by making reference to what he deems to be biblical "paradoxes,"[38] "ambiguities,"[39] and "enigmas"[40] in regard to the matter. He even

---

35. The report clearly states its abstentionist character: On page 33 the committee "reaffirms its advocacy of total abstinence from the beverage use of alcohol," Gilchrist.

36. *Ibid.*, p. 23.

37. Lindsell, p. 116. Emphasis mine. In effect he has declared that the Scriptures are not adequate today to equip us for every good work, contrary to 2 Timothy 3:16–17. This is a "holier than thou" position with a vengeance: it is "holier" than Scripture itself!

38. Reynolds, pp. 8–10. Indeed, his actual study of the issue before us opens with these words: "There are paradoxes in the Bible about a number of matters," p. 8.

39. *Ibid.*, pp. 21, 36.

40. *Ibid.*, pp. 36–37.

asserts that God "left a number of things somewhat difficult to perceive as a test of the spiritual perception of Bible readers."[41] Reynolds adds: "In the same way God may have left His true teaching concerning alcoholic beverages with what the undiscerning find to be ambiguities."[42]

Indeed, in the opinion of Reynolds, it is probably the case that

> God may place these enigmas in the Bible here and there to make believers search diligently. . . .
>
> In the same way He may have left the teaching concerning the command to total abstinence somewhat obscure as a test to determine who among those who profess to believe in Him would discern His true meaning.[43]

But then again, maybe he did not! Maybe God meant what he said!

The New Testament and Alcohol Use

The New Testament is only about one-third the size of the Old Testament. Its historical scope—covering the period from the birth of Christ in 4 B.C. until the completion of the last New Testament book—spans only 75 to 100 years.[44] In contrast, the Old Testament material spans history from the creation (c. 10,000 B.C.?) until around 400 B.C. (excluding prophetic statements regarding the eschatological future), although the Old Testament canon itself dates from 1450 B.C. to 400 B.C. Furthermore, the Old Testament is clearly foundational for and

41. *Ibid.*, p. 21.
42. *Ibid.*
43. *Ibid.*, p. 36.
44. There is some renewed debate over whether the last canonical book of the New Testament was written prior to A.D. 70 (the dominant view in biblical scholarship until the 1800s) or around A.D. 95 (the prevailing view of the last one hundred years). For a compelling defense of this very "conservative" early date, see *Redating the New Testament* by the otherwise very liberal scholar John A. T. Robinson (Philadelphia: Westminster Press, 1976).

preparational to the New Testament in every sense of the word. In light of these factors of size, dates, and function, it should not be surprising that the material of the Old Testament relating to our study is much more abundant than that of the New Testament. However, in light of the fundamental unity of the two Testaments (e.g., Matt. 5:17–19; 1 Cor. 10:11), the Old Testament is as binding and ethically relevant (2 Tim. 3:16–17) as that of the New Testament, unless the New specifically repeals a principle or practice of the Old (as in the case of the sacrificial system, cf. Hebrews).

Consequently, our study of the New Testament will be somewhat shorter than the foregoing. Nevertheless, it will be shown that the New Testament in no way contravenes the Old in regard to the matter of alcohol and is, in fact, perfectly harmonious with it. Let us now turn to consideration of two important Greek terms relevant to our study.

oinos

This word occurs 33 times in the New Testament and is consistently translated "wine." It also occurs in various compounds such as *oinophlugia* ("excess wine"), *paroinos* ("addicted to wine"), and *oinopotēs* ("drunkard"). There is a clear interpretive consensus from a variety of angles as to the fermented quality of *oinos*.

First, *oinos* is the Greek equivalent to the Hebrew *yayin*, which has been shown to be fermented wine.[45] Biblical lexicographers (e.g., J. H. Thayer[46] and G. Abbott-Smith[47]) point to its frequent use in the Septuagint as a translation for *yayin*. Second, classical Greek—the historical forerunner of New Testament (*koine*) Greek—employs the term as a fermented beverage. The Liddell and Scott *Greek-English Lexicon* of classical Greek defines *oinos* as "the fermented juice of the grape."[48] Interestingly, clas-

---

45. Cf. pp. 29ff. *supra.* Note references to Easton, Moore, and Davis.

46. Joseph Henry Thayer, *A Greek-English Lexicon of the New Testament* (New York: American Book Co., 1889), p. 442.

47. G. Abbott-Smith, *A Manual Greek Lexicon of the New Testament* (Edinburgh: T & T Clark, rep. 1950), p. 314: "in LXX chiefly for *yayin*."

48. Henry George Liddell and Robert Scott, *A Greek-English Lexicon*, 5th ed. (Oxford: Clarendon Press, 1864), p. 976.

sical Greek apparently used *oinos* as a functional equivalent for "fermented juice," as Liddell and Scott note:

> . . . also the fermented juice of other kinds, *oinos ek krithōn* barley-*wine*, a kind of *beer* . . . *palm-wine* . . . *lotus-wine* . . .—from which drinks *grape-wine*, *oinos ampelinos*, is expressly distinguished.[49]

Third, Greek New Testament lexicographers maintain its fermented quality. The standard lexicon of our day, Arndt-Gingrich, notes that the word is "normally the fermented juice of the grape . . . the word for 'must, or unfermented grape juice,' is *trux*."[50] The reputable *Illustrated Davis Bible Dictionary* agrees: "The Greek *oinos* . . . means the fermented juice of the grape, except when it is qualified by the word 'new.' "[51] No major New Testament lexicon disputes the fermented character of *oinos*.

Not only is there clear lexical evidence to the alcoholic nature of *oinos*, but there is clear New Testament contextual evidence as well. In Ephesians 5:18 Paul exhorts the Ephesian Christians (and all Christians) to "be not drunk with wine, wherein is excess . . ." (KJV). In Paul's prerequisites for church leadership he commands that "Deacons likewise must be men of dignity, not double-tongued, or *addicted* to much wine" (1 Tim. 3:8, italics added), and that "older women likewise are to be reverent in their behavior, not malicious gossips, not *enslaved* to much wine . . ." (Titus 2:3, italics added). These statements imply the alcoholic nature of *oinos* beyond a shadow of doubt.

The case is clear: *oinos* is an alcoholic beverage. Yet nowhere is wine *per se* forbidden; nowhere is there established a prohibition in regard to its consumption. As a matter of fact, as already hinted at above, even ordained church officers are not required to abstain from enjoyment of it. The specific requirement relative to wine use among officer candidates is that which is characteristic of the moderationist position.

49. *Ibid.*
50. W. F. Arndt and F. W. Gingrich, *A Greek-English Lexicon of the New Testament* (Chicago: University of Chicago Press, 1957), p. 564.
51. Davis, *Dictionary*, p. 867.

In 1 Timothy 3:3 and Titus 1:7 the requirement for the office of elder is that the candidate be "not addicted to wine." In 1 Timothy 3:8 the obligation for the office of deacon is that the candidate be not "addicted to much wine." In the former case the word used is *paroinos*, of which Thayer notes it refers to "one who sits long at his wine, *given to wine, drunken.*"[52] In the latter case the words employed are *mē oinō pollō prosechontas* (literally: "not wine much devoted to," i.e., "not devoted to much wine").[53] The reference to "much" (*pollō*) and "devoted" (*prosechontas*) are both important. "Much" deals with the amount of intake; "devoted" speaks of the inordinate, immoderate attachment to wine. It is quite significant that Paul refrains from a total prohibition for officers of the church. He only forbids *abuse* of alcoholic beverages. (Who could say he was commanding that officers not be "devoted to much" grape juice?) No New Testament apostle ever commands anything along the lines of: "Drink no wine at all." The commands are clearly along the lines of: "Be not *drunk* with wine" (Eph. 5:18); "Be not addicted to much wine" (1 Tim. 3:8); "Be not enslaved to wine" (Titus 2:3); and so on.

An interesting but ultimately futile attempt is made by some prohibitionists to *eis*egetically argue that Paul speaks of wine as something evil itself. Reynolds is a case in point:

> "Be not drunk with wine in which is debauchery." Some commentators say that the words "in which" refer to the whole phrase, "Be not drunk with wine," and not just to "wine." The wish not to accept the idea that debauchery is "in" wine makes them reject this obvious sense, and choose instead the idea that it lies in being drunk.[54]

The obvious problem with such a statement immediately arises, as mentioned above. Why did Paul not simply say, "*Drink* no wine, wherein is excess"? Why does he persistently add such

52. Thayer, p. 490.
53. Arndt-Gingrich, p. 721. *Prosechontas* means *"occupy oneself with, devote or apply oneself to."* It is used again in 1 Timothy 4:13 of devoting oneself to ministerial duties, q.v.
54. Reynolds, p. 53.

limiting notions to the act of drinking, such as drunkenness, addiction, and long-lingering?

gleukos

This word occurs only once in the New Testament, in Acts 2:13. According to Thayer, it means *"must,* the sweet juice pressed from the grape . . . *sweet wine."*[55] It is strange that this word, which *probably*[56] refers only to unfermented beverage, occurs only once. Why is it not commended and *oinos* forbidden? This hapaxlegomenon is not significant to our study, except in this limited, inferential way.

Jesus and Wine

The Lord Jesus Christ lived in a culture that used wine (which, as has been shown, could intoxicate) as a common, everyday beverage.[57] Although he spoke out against drunkenness as a sinful condition (Matt. 24:29; Luke 12:45; 21:34), Jesus *never* disparaged the drinking of wine (*oinos*) *per se.* As a matter of biblical fact, he would then have not only been at variance with the Old Testament (which he affirmed as the unfailing Word of God), but he would also have been guilty of hypocrisy. This may be seen in that:

1. *Jesus himself drank wine.* As a matter of fact, in Luke 7:33–35 he makes reference to his practice of drinking wine as a vivid illustration of a distinctive difference between himself and his forerunner, John the Baptist:

> [Jesus said:] "For John the Baptist has come eating no bread and drinking no wine; and you say, 'He has a demon!' The Son of Man has come eating and drinking; and you say, 'Behold, a gluttonous man, and a drunkard, a friend of tax-gatherers and sinners.' Yet wisdom is vindicated by all her children."

55. Thayer, p. 118.
56. The insertion of the tentative "probably" is necessary because in its only occurrence in the New Testament it is used in an allegation that the disciples were drunk on it, cf. Acts 2:13. Many lexicographers say that it could well include fermented wine in its connotation. See references alluding to this passage elsewhere in this work.
57. Alfred Edersheim, *The Life and Times of Jesus the Messiah* (Grand Rapids: Eerdmans, 1972), Book 4, chapter 12.

There are some who maintain that this citation does not state that Jesus did, in fact, drink wine. Particular emphasis is placed on the fact that although "wine" is specifically mentioned in reference to John (that is, Jesus mentions that John avoids it), the reference to Jesus' drinking omits the word *wine*. However, this attempt to avoid the obvious is unsuccessful for two reasons:

First, there is widespread agreement among commentators that there is an obvious intended parallel in the two statements that demands that "wine" be understood to be assumed in the second part of the statement. The accusation against Jesus is intended to be an antithetic parallelism, a thought being expressed by contrasting it with its opposite. Here the contrast is between *not* "eating and drinking" and "eating and drinking." Second, were it the case that Jesus did *not* drink wine, how could it be alleged that he was a drunkard? Why did he not point out that they were mistaken in their assertion that he drank?

Reynolds admits the parallelism but maintains that the contrast was over John's "Naziritic" abstinence from "non-alcoholic products of the grape"[58] and Jesus' partaking of such. This assertion is tenuous, at best. In the first place, it is only a conjecture, based on slight intimation and accidental similarity that John was a Nazirite. There is no statement as to his being a "Nazirite" in the biblical record. In the allegedly similar case of Samson, it is specifically stated that Samson was to "be a Nazirite to God from the womb . . ." (Judg. 13:7). In the Gospel records such a statement is conspicuously absent. Furthermore, there is no mention of any other of the Naziritic strictures that were revealed in Numbers 6. For instance, there is no requirement forbidding John's parents to cut his hair (compare Num. 6:5 with Judg. 13:5). Neither do we discover a record of the Baptist's having long hair in the several descriptions of him (Matt. 3:4; 11:8; Mark 1:6).

In the second place, the angelic revelation given John's father in Luke 1:15 only restricts him from partaking of "wine" (*oinos*) and "strong drink" (*sikera*). In light of the immediate context,

58. Reynolds, p. 39.

the practice seems to be designed to encourage his having a special infilling of the Holy Spirit (compare v. 15b with Eph. 5:18). He is not forbidden "must" (*trux*) or "sweet new wine" (*gleukos*). And it is the wine matter that is particularly mentioned by Christ in Luke 7 as the point of concern.

Furthermore, Jesus does employ the term *oinos*, which is clearly alcoholic. Jesus admitted to drinking *oinos*. He was not accused of becoming drunk on grape juice!

2. *Jesus miraculously "manufactured" a high-quality wine at Cana in Galilee* (John 2:1-11). The quantity was upwards of six firkins (about 120 gallons) for the wedding party and guests.

Some have objected to the use of this miracle in support of the moderationist argument. It has been argued by some that both the wine that ran out and the miraculously produced wine were actually grape juice. But this is in defiance of the facts: First, the word *oinos* is used in reference to both wines in question. It has been shown that this word indicates fermented-quality grape drink, i.e., wine. Second, William Hendriksen has commented that due to the season of the wedding—just before Spring Passover (cf. John 2:13)—the wine must have been fermented. The grape harvest had been collected over six months earlier, in September. Thus, the wine had ample time to ferment.[59]

Reynolds, however, in his characteristically innovative style, interprets the occasion along wholly different lines:

> The situation appears to have been as follows: The wedding party had been indulging in cheap, foul tasting wine, made perhaps partly from diseased grapes, and having a high alcoholic content. The people were drunk and behaving in a manner which moved to righteous indignation our Lord who was and is absolutely and totally pure of mind and body. His mother's sorrow that the party had run out of that sort of wine and her implied suggestion that He provide more of the same caused Him in righteous sorrow to speak stern words to her which have much puzzled Bible commentators.[60]

59. William Hendriksen, *New Testament Commentary: John* (Grand Rapids: Baker, 1973), p. 115.
60. Reynolds, pp. 37-38.

Stripped of the imaginative conjecture about wine from diseased grapes, his case is basically established upon the following considerations[61]: (a) Jesus severely rebuked his mother (v. 4), indicating his displeasure at her bringing him to such a riotous feast; (b) based on verse 10 in the Greek, "the people at the wedding party were already intoxicated"; (c) the governor of the feast who "had surely not become drunk" recognized the new drink as the "best wine (grape juice). . . . This he said as a connoisseur of choice vintage without regard to alcoholic content," according to Reynolds (p. 38); and (d) with so much drunkenness involved, it would be morally intolerable for Christ to have provided such a large quantity of alcoholic wine.

In consideration of the merits of Reynolds's thought-provoking argument, it should be noted in the first place that his interpretation of Jesus' rebuke of Mary is questionable. Commentators have inconclusively debated the rationale of the rebuke throughout Christian history. Not only so, but Reynolds's interpretation implicates Mary in a grossly sinful tolerance of radically evil conduct. This is quite out of character for her in terms of the biblical record elsewhere. Furthermore, it is even out of character for Jesus. Why is there no rebuke for those who were drunk? Or for the governor of such a feast? Why did Jesus do anything at all to assist them in their riotous party? Why did he stay around until the wine ran out?

Still further, why did Mary immediately (v. 5) urge the servants to prepare for some miracle (or otherwise respond positively to her plea) from Christ in light of such an alleged rebuke? A more plausible interpretation of Jesus' rebuke is that he was just beginning his messianic (cf. John 2:11) ministry, and it was now time for Mary to cease looking upon him as her son and to begin recognizing him as her Lord and Savior.[62]

In the second place, Reynolds seems to both misinterpret and misapply the governor's statement and to overstate his own lexical case. It must be noted that the governor does *not* say that those at this particular party are "drunk." Rather, he is stating

61. Taken from *ibid.*, pp. 37–39.
62. Hendriksen, *John*, p. 115.

a general practice among those who host feasts: "Every man serves the good wine first, and when men have drunk freely, then that which is poorer. . . ." Many commentators see this as does J. C. Ellicott: "There is clearly no reference to the present feast. It is a coarse jest of the ruler's, the sort of remark that forms part of the stock in trade of a hired manager of banquets."[63]

In addition it should be noted that the Greek text does not demand the translation urged by Reynolds (although it is lexically possible). Reynolds says in regard to the term *methusthosin* in verse 10:

> There is little to support the idea that this is not said in reference to the wedding party, or that it does not mean that they were intoxicated.[64]
>
> [And further:] From the expressions used in modern English translations it might be understood that the wedding party had drunk enough to remove some of their thirst, but were still sober and were behaving decorously. The Greek word *methuō* does not allow such an interpretation. Liddell and Scott's highly respected *Greek English Lexicon* says it means "to be drunken". . . . In no passage in the Bible or out of it does it mean to have quenched the thirst while remaining sober.[65]

Not only does Reynolds by his own admission set himself against the consensus of "modern English translations," but he apparently has not carefully researched the matter. It is true that the *methuō* word group is generally to be translated in a way to indicate drunkenness; this is its preponderate and primary usage. But this is not its only meaning or function, contrary to Reynolds's sweeping assertion.

The standard Arndt-Gingrich lexicon notes under the *methuskō* entry that it can mean "drink freely" and lists John 2:10 as a

---

63. John Charles Ellicott, ed., *The Four Gospels*, in *Ellicott's Commentary on the Whole Bible* (Grand Rapids: Zondervan, rep. 1954), VI:394. Cf. Adam Clarke, *Clarke's Commentary* (Nashville: Abingdon, n.d.), V:527. Robert Trench, *Notes on the Miracles and Parables of Our Lord* (Old Tappan, NJ: Revell, 1953), I:117.

64. Reynolds, p. 37.

65. *Ibid.*, pp. 38–39.

demonstration of that usage. Linguist Herbert Preisker in the authoritative *Theological Dictionary of the New Testament* makes the following observations on this word group and on John 2:10 in particular:

> *Methuskō* can often be used for a refreshing drink [as in Greek literature] "I will refresh the souls of the priests."[66]
> [And he adds further:] Philo commends *methē* and *methuein* for the wise man as the drinking of wine, not to excess (*adēn*) nor unmixed (*akraton*) . . . but with moderation and joy.[67]

Then Preisker approaches the passage in question:

> *Methuō* and *methuskomai* are mostly used lit[erally] in the NT for "to be drunk" and "to get drunk". *Methuskomai* is used with no ethical or religious judgment in Jn. 2:10 in connection with the rule that the poorer wine is served only when the guests have drunk well.[68]

Other technical lexical tools cite the Septuagint usage of the *methuō* word group in various Old Testament passages as illustrative of this fact. For instance, the Parkhurst lexicon is very clear:

> *Methuō* . . . It denotes in general to drink wine or strong drink more freely than usual, and that whether to drunkenness or not. . . . Pass[ively] To drink freely and to cheerfulness, though not to drunkenness . . . John 2:10. And in this sense the verb is plainly used by the LXX [i.e. Septuagint], Gen. 43:34; Cant. 5:1; and also, I think, in Gen. 9:21. . . .[69]

Finally, Reynolds's statement regarding the governor's acting as a "connoisseur of choice vintage without regard to alcoholic

66. Herbert Preisker in Gerhard Kittel, *Theological Dictionary of the New Testament* (Grand Rapids: Eerdmans, 1967), IV:546.

67. *Ibid.*

68. *Ibid.*, p. 547.

69. John Parkhurst, *A Greek and English Lexicon to the New Testament*, 7th ed. (London: Thomas Davison, Whitefriars, 1817), p. 422.

content" is purely gratuitous and is based on preconceived ideas imported into the text. It further goes against the well-nigh universal prevalence of men to prefer old (fermented) wine over new (pre- or unfermented) wine. The Lord himself makes reference to this assessment among men in Luke 5:39: "And no one, after drinking old wine wishes for new; for he says, 'The old is good enough.' " Seeseman notes that such an assessment was prevalent among Jewish writers (cf. Sir. 9:10; Ber. 51a), as well as Greek and Roman authors (cf. Lucianus, *De Mercede Conductis*, 26; Plutarchus, *De Mario*, 44; Plautus, *Casina*, 5).[70]

Even Messianic prophecies use the imagery of "aged" (old, fermented) wine at banquets as illustrative of that which is good. Isaiah 25:6 says:

> And the LORD of hosts will prepare a lavish banquet for all
> peoples on this mountain;
> A banquet of aged wine, choice pieces with marrow,
> And refined, aged wine.

It is upon this basis that the governor's statement must be understood—"you have kept the good wine until now." Both the original wine and the miraculously produced wine are called *oinos*, which means "fermented grape juice," or alcoholic wine.

Communion Wine

The Last Supper was instituted with wine—not grape juice. This is easily demonstrated in light of both exegetical and cultural considerations.

It is true that Jesus is consistently recorded as having spoken of "the cup" as filled with "the fruit of the vine" (Matt. 26:29; Mark 14:25; Luke 22:18). Generally the opponents of wine use in communion services fail to recognize that this term was a functional equivalent for "wine." If taken literally, the phrase would lead to an absurdity: it would teach that the cup was filled with whole grapes! However, the observations from the following authorities should help clear up this mistaken notion.

70. Heinrich Seeseman in Kittel, *TDNT* (1967) V:163.

Dunlop Moore has written:

> The expression the "fruit of the vine" is employed by our
> Saviour in the synoptical Gospels to denote the element con-
> tained in the cup of the Holy Supper. The fruit of the vine is
> literally the grape. But the Jews from time immemorial have used
> this phrase to designate the wine partaken of on sacred occasions,
> as at the Passover and on the evening of the Sabbath. The
> Mishna (De. Bened, cap. 6, pars i) expressly states, that, in pro-
> nouncing blessings, "the fruit of the vine" is the consecrated
> expression for yayin. . . . The Christian Fathers, as well as the
> Jewish rabbis, have understood "the fruit of the vine" to mean
> wine in the proper sense. Our Lord, in instituting the Supper
> after the Passover, availed himself of the expression invariably
> employed by his countrymen in speaking of the wine of the Pass-
> over. On other occasions, when employing the language of com-
> mon life, he calls wine by its ordinary name.[71]

Davis's dictionary agrees:

> Fruit of the vine, the designation used by Jesus at the insti-
> tution of the Lord's Supper . . . is the expression employed by
> the Jews from time immemorial for the wine partaken of on
> sacred occasions, as at the passover and on the evening of the
> Sabbath (Mishna, Berakoth, vi. 1). The Greeks also used the
> term as a synonym of wine which was capable of producing in-
> toxication (Herod i. 211, 212).[72]

Heinrich Seesemann notes of the phrase "fruit of the vine":

> It is obvious . . . that according to custom Jesus was proffering
> wine in the cup over which He pronounced the blessing; this
> may be seen especially from the solemn genēma tēs ampelou . . .
> which was borrowed from Judaism.[73]

71. Moore, "Wine," in Schaff, Encyclopedia, pp. 2537, 2538.
72. Davis, Dictionary, p. 868.
73. Seeseman, in Kittel, TDNT, V:164.

For additional information along these lines, consult the following scholars: Friedrich Buschel, Johannes Behm, and G. Dalman.[74] This may be helpful in explaining the problem of drunkenness at communion services in the troublesome Corinthian church (1 Cor. 11:21–22).[75]

As with concluding the survey of the Old Testament, we close this study of the New Testament evidence with a telling admission by an abstentionist publication: "From the example and teaching of Jesus and the teaching of Paul, it cannot be certainly concluded that total abstinence was a requirement in the New Testament church."[76]

Alleged Negative Passages

Before moving on into the matter of Christian liberty, which is more directly related to the abstentionist position, it may be helpful to consider the passages allegedly undermining the moderationist argument.

There are several biblical passages that upon cursory reading may seem to imply that all wine drinking is prohibited. That these observations are in error should be apparent in light of the integrity of Scripture. Ample exegetical evidence drawn from a wide array of passages has been rehearsed above and has conclusively demonstrated the contrary. Below will be listed eight of the more prominent passages that are employed in the argument for total abstinence. Explanatory statements will be offered to show that these passages perfectly harmonize with the passages previously explored.

Leviticus 10:8–11

The LORD then spoke to Aaron, saying, "Do not drink wine or strong drink, neither you nor your sons with you, when you

74. Friedrich Buschel in Kittel *TDNT*, (1964), I:685; Johannes Behm, in *ibid.* (1965), 3:733ff.; G Dalman, *Arbeit v. Sitte in Palastina*, iv (1935), p. 137.

75. It is significant to note that even in light of their drunkenness, Paul does *not* issue a "cease and desist" order in this matter.

76. Gilchrist, p. 25.

come into the tent of meeting, so that you may not die—it is a perpetual statute throughout your generations—and so as to make a distinction between the holy and profane, and between the unclean and the clean, and so as to teach the sons of Israel all the statutes which the LORD has spoken to them through Moses."

This passage clearly institutes as a "perpetual statute" that members of the Aaronic priesthood should not drink alcoholic beverages when they enter the tabernacle. However, relative to the use of this passage in the context of the present debate, it must be noted that this prohibition is restricted to the priest in the priesthood (Aaron and his sons), and it only forbade the use of alcoholic beverages when actually engaging in the priestly function.

Apparently this was enacted as a safety valve for the priesthood, to prevent any accidental profanation of the tabernacle service. The context seems to demand such an interpretation, for in verse 1 we read:

Now Nadab and Abihu, the sons of Aaron, took their respective firepans, and after putting fire in them, placed incense on it and offered strange fire before the LORD, which He had not commanded them.

Verses 2 and 3 give the result of such a profanation of the priestly function and God's reason for such severe punishment:

And fire came out from the presence of the LORD and consumed them, and they died before the LORD. Then Moses said to Aaron, "It is what the LORD spoke, saying,

'By those who come near Me I will be treated as holy, And before all the people I will be honored.' "

So Aaron, therefore, kept silent.

Nadab and Abihu had offered things on the altar not commanded by God. Consequently, the priest must be extremely careful that he follow God's stipulations in his service. Were the priest to be allowed to drink just before or during a priestly service, his mind might not carefully follow God's order of service. This passage has nothing to do with us today, since we are not of the Aaronic priesthood, which has passed away (cf. Hebrews 9 and 10).

Despite these observations, some have argued that this prohibition remains incumbent upon New Testament era believers because they are "kings and priests" (cf. e.g., 1 Peter 2:5, 9; Rev. 1:6). Two representatives of this strained but widespread position will be cited. One is prohibitionist Stephen Reynolds; the other is an abstentionist, Gleason L. Archer. In Reynolds's case the focus is not on the present passage, but on Proverbs 31:4–5, which forbids kings to drink. However, the manner and assumptions of the arguments of both men are the same.

Upon making reference to Revelation 1:6 (which teaches that believers are "kings and priests"), Reynolds states:

> It follows, if we accept this reading [i.e., the Textus Receptus], that all Bible believers must be abstainers, since what was required of kings in the Old Testament is required of kings under the New.
>
> [In the next paragraph he adds:] If ancient kings were warned not to drink intoxicants lest they forget the law, modern believers who wish to keep God's law in their heart, should accept this prohibition as binding on themselves.[77]

In a similar vein, and with an identical spiritual *non sequitur*, Archer informs us that:

> This has implications for the New Testament priesthood of all believers (1 Peter 2:9) and suggests that they may be seriously handicapped in carrying on the work of soulwinning if they personally indulge in the use of alcohol.[78]

77. Reynolds, p. 34.
78. Archer, *Encyclopedia*, p. 148.

This methodology is beset with a number of problems. A few brief observations will demonstrate the spurious nature of such an application of Scripture:

First, if such methodology were proper, both of these provisions (relative to both priest and king) would witness against our High Priest and King of kings, Jesus Christ. As shown previously, Jesus did partake of wine. Given the integrity of Scripture, this evidence alone exposes the argument's *reductio ad absurdum.*

Second, even in the Old Testament this spiritual truth (that believers are kings and priests) was true. The Old Testament background for both 1 Peter 2:5, 9 and Revelation 1:6 is Exodus 19:6, which says: "You shall be a *kingdom* of *priests*" (italics added). Yet the Old Testament is clear that Israelites were permitted wine.

Third, both the priestly and kingly prohibitions have implied limitations; i.e., the prohibition was in effect during the actual exercise of the powers of office. Leviticus 10:9 particularly commands: "Do not drink wine or strong drink . . . when you come into the tent of meeting. . . ." Such an implication is strongly present in the rationale for the prohibition given in Proverbs 31:5, which clearly states in this regard: "Lest they drink and forget what is decreed, and pervert the rights of all the afflicted." The perversion of rights could only come about with official sanction, i.e., while acting magisterially. The prohibition was given in order to forestall the frequent corruption of justice brought about by kings who functioned magisterially under the influence of alcohol (e.g., Isa. 28:7). Wine was not forbidden to kings permanently and universally (cf. Gen. 14:18–20).

The most that can be said of such an argument is that while in the process of carrying on the work of soulwinning, the believer should not drink! The moderationist would follow this principle in his personal witness without argument.

Fourth, if such a hermeneutic were allowed, what sense could be made of Paul's requirement for the eldership and diaconate? Earlier we discussed how the prerequisites were specifically stated to exclude only those "addicted to much wine" (1 Tim. 3:8) and those "addicted to wine" (v. 3). Furthermore, what sense could be made of Paul's "Be not drunk with wine"? Why did he not say, "Do not drink wine"?

Other objections to such an employment of Leviticus 10 and Proverbs 31 could be marshaled against Reynolds and Archer. But space prohibits delving further into the matter. The above should be sufficient, despite its brevity.

Numbers 6:2–6

[The LORD said to Moses:] "Speak to the sons of Israel, and say to them, 'When a man or woman makes a special vow, the vow of a Nazirite, to dedicate himself to the LORD, he shall abstain from wine and strong drink; he shall drink no vinegar, whether made from wine or strong drink, neither shall he drink any grape juice, nor eat fresh or dried grapes. All the days of his separation he shall not eat anything that is produced by the grape vine, from the seeds even to the skin. All the days of his vow of separation no razor shall pass over his head. He shall be holy until the days are fulfilled for which he separated himself to the LORD; he shall let the locks of hair on his head grow long. All the days of his separation to the LORD he shall not go near to a dead person.' "

Again here is another clear prohibition to wine drinking. But again this is a special circumstance totally irrelevant to our standing and conduct today. This prohibition was a piece of Naziritic legislation that (1) forbade wine only after a peculiar, public vow was taken (v. 2); (2) included avoidance of all grapes (v. 3), cutting of hair (v. 5), and contact with a dead body (v. 6); and (3) was only a temporary abstinence: "Then the priest shall wave them for a wave offering before the LORD. It is holy for the priest, together with the breast offered by waving and the thigh offered by lifting up; and afterward the Nazirite may drink wine" (v. 20).

Judges 13:4

[The angel of the LORD said:] "Now therefore, be careful not to drink wine or strong drink, nor eat any unclean thing."

Since this command is quite particular and limited, its universal application would be a travesty of exposition. Verses 2 and 3 inform the attentive reader that this command was given to Manoah's wife, whose circumstances were unique. She was forbidden wine because she was to conceive a very special child, Samson, who was to be "a Nazirite unto God from the womb . . ." (v. 5).

Proverbs 20:1

> Wine is a mocker, strong drink a brawler.
> And whoever is intoxicated by it is not wise.

Although not tied to unique circumstance, this verse is not a universal prohibition to wine drinking. The statement refers to the inebriating *potential* of wine and strong drink, of which the user must be wary. It is a warning to those who use it immoderately. Note the following observations:

First: the warning pattern. The warning "wine is a mocker" follows the pattern of 1 Corinthians 8:1, which says that "knowledge makes arrogant. . . ." It should be obvious that neither Christian ethics nor a biblical world-view disparage the quest for knowledge as a proper function of rational beings. In this respect—how men employ them—wine and knowledge are similar in that they can each be used for either good or evil. The point of the Proverbs writer is that wine has the *potential* to mock, just as the point of Paul is that knowledge has the potential to make arrogant.

Second: warning specifics. By a perspicuous statement, this warning is tied to the issue of the *abuse* of wine, not just by analogy. Delitzsch's comments on this passage are very much to the point:

> Wine is a mocker, because he who is intoxicated with it readily scoffs at that which is holy; mead is boisterous . . . because he who is inebriated in his dissolute madness breaks through the limits of morality and propriety. He is unwise who, through wine and the like, i.e. overpowered by it (cf. 2 Sam. 13:28), staggers, i.e. he gives himself up to wine to such a degree that he is no longer master of himself.[79]

79. Franz Delitzsch, *Proverbs* in C. F. Keil and Franz Delitzsch, *Commentary on the Old Testament* (Grand Rapids: Eerdmans, rep. 1978), II:39.

He adds that "the passionate slavish desire of wine or for wine" is what is referred to here. This is why the statement "wine is a mocker, strong drink a brawler" is followed immediately by the comment that "he who is *intoxicated* by it is not wise."

Third: the warning context. The biblical interpreter must not be selective in his approach to Scripture. Verses must not be divorced from their wider contexts and the whole system of biblical ethics. The mass of evidence rehearsed heretofore is overwhelmingly supportive of the moderationist position. God gives "wine which makes man's heart glad" (Ps. 104:15). Wine is a reward of rejoicing for obedience to God (Deut. 14:26ff.). Wine, which in the drunkard's life is a "brawler," is in the poetry of God an emblem of messianic blessing (e.g., Amos 9:13–15).

Proverbs 21:17
> He who loves pleasure will become a poor man;
> He who loves wine and oil will not become rich.

This statement is wrongly used if employed in support of total abstinence or prohibition. The verse refers to a constant, inordinate seeking of wine to the neglect of labor and other godly virtues. It should be noticed that the writer does not mention the love of wine alone. Also mentioned is the love of oil. Is oil, then, an element to be avoided? Obviously not (e.g., Ps. 104:15). This proverb merely urges the godly to keep things in perspective. If the love of money is a root of evil (1 Tim. 6:10), is money, then, to be abstained from? Or is it the *love* of money that is the issue? He that has ears to hear, let him hear.

Proverbs 23:31–32
> Do not look upon the wine when it is red,
> When it sparkles in the cup,
> When it goes down smoothly;
> At the last it bites like a serpent,
> And stings like a viper.

Undoubtedly this passage is one of the most frequently employed texts in the debate over wine drinking. Indeed, prohibitionist Reynolds in his *Alcohol and the Bible* not only opens his major argument (p. 9) with this passage, but closes his book with reference to it (p. 64). It may be fairly stated that, according to Reynolds and those of like persuasion, this passage is *the* most significant and compelling prohibitionist statement in Scripture.[80] Before interpreting the passage, then, it will be helpful to cite some of Reynolds's observations on it.

In a section entitled "The Absolute Prohibition of Proverbs 23:29–31" the following comments are found:

> It is true that hyperboles occur in the Bible, but one cannot read Proverbs 23:29–35 without coming to the conclusion that God is speaking of something He loathes as an article for human consumption. There is no suggestion that a good thing which He has given to us to enjoy is in view here. It is viper's poison (verse 32) and the command is not to look on it.[81]

Reynolds then argues from what he deems to be a parallel situation. He observes that when Lot was leaving Sodom, he was forbidden to look back upon the city (Gen. 19:17ff). This was due to the moral evil that infested Sodom. Hence there is the absolute prohibition by God. Thus, God "also put an absolute prohibition on looking at a certain sort of *yayin* (Prov. 23:31). . . . The prohibition is absolute, like that of looking at Sodom. . . ."[82]

In Reynolds's view, the absolute prohibition is here—and not at other references to *yayin*—because the wine is specifically designated as "red." The idea behind this "red" designation is that it is alcoholic and causes redness of eyes and nose when indulged in.[83] Thus, he concludes: "It is puerile to suppose this command is not to be taken seriously and that the prohibition

---

80. Reynolds, p. 61, says: "It is the intent of this essay to prove that Proverbs teaches an absolute prohibition against the beverage use of alcohol. . . ."

81. *Ibid.*, p. 10.

82. *Ibid.*, p. 11.

83. *Ibid.*, p. 12.

is not absolute. All the prohibitions of Proverbs 23 are absolute."[84]

Reynolds has some intriguing arguments based on lexical considerations supportive of his view that "red" indicates "alcoholic."[85] And he *may* well be correct in this observation. However, this point can be conceded without at all altering the moderationist argument in the least. Let us make some observations on the substance of his argument from Proverbs 23:

1. This passage has to be utterly divorced from its near, far, and ultimate contexts to bear the construction put upon it. The near (immediate) context is extremely clear: the warning and admonition are specifically applied to immoderate abusers of wine. Let us cite the whole passage in demonstration of this:

29. Who has woe? Who has sorrow?
    Who has contentions? Who has complaining?
    Who has wounds without cause?
    Who has redness of eyes?
30. Those who linger long over wine,
    Those who go to taste mixed wine.
31. Do not look on the wine when it is red,
    When it sparkles in the cup,
    When it goes down smoothly;
32. At the last it bites like a serpent,
    And stings like a viper.
33. Your eyes will see strange things,
    And your mind will utter perverse things.
34. And you will be like one who lies down in the middle of the sea,
    Or like one who lies down on the top of a mast.
35. "They struck me, but I did not become ill;
    They beat me, but I did not know it.
    When shall I awake?
    I will seek another drink."

How could a context be any clearer? Here is specifically and carefully described a person to whom the admonition is directed.

84. *Ibid.*, p. 64.
85. *Ibid.*, pp. 11–14, 63–64.

He exhibits all the emotional, social, and physical characteristics of the drunkard: depression (v. 29a), a contentious spirit (v. 29b), and telltale physical appearance. (v. 29c). Here we have before our view those who "linger long over wine" (v. 30). These drunkards have developed alcohol-induced delusions (v. 33), disorientation (v. 34), and detachment (v. 35a, b). But despite all this, such a one addicted to wine refuses to give it up (v. 35c).

The far context is almost as helpful. In verses 20–21 we are prepared for the warning of verse 31:

20. Do not be with heavy drinkers of wine,
    Or with gluttonous eaters of meat;
21. For the heavy drinker and the glutton will come to poverty,
    And drowsiness will clothe a man with rags.

Finally, the ultimate context is the entire Scripture, which clearly does not forbid the moderate partaking of "aged wine" (Isa. 25:6), "strong drink" (Deut. 14:26), or "all sorts of wine" (Neh. 5:18). The "gladdening effect" of wine is acceptable, at least to some degree, according to several passages (Ps. 104:15; Eccles. 9:7; 10:19; 2 Sam. 13:28; Esther 1:10; Zech. 9:15; 10:7; Judg. 9:13).

2. Reynolds distorts a figure involved in the passage. The text does not say, "*It* is a viper's poison."[86] It says, "at the last it bites *like* a serpent, and stings *like* an adder" (v. 32). There is a world of difference between reality ("is") and analogy ("is like"). It is "at the last"—after "lingering long"—that it can be harmful, "like" a viper. It is the *abuse* that is in view here, not the *use*.

In this respect it is somewhat similar to Isaiah 1, which reads:

10. Hear the word of the LORD,
    You rulers of Sodom;
    Give ear to the instruction of our God,
    You people of Gomorrah.
11. "What are your multiplied sacrifices to Me?"
    Says the LORD.

86. *Ibid.,* p. 10. Cp. p. 30.

"I have had enough of burnt offerings of rams,
And the fat of fed cattle.
And I take no pleasure in the blood of bulls, lambs, or goats.
12. "When you come to appear before Me,
Who requires of you this trampling of My courts?
13. "Bring your worthless offerings no longer,
Incense is an abomination to Me.
New moon and sabbath, the calling of assemblies—
I cannot endure iniquity and the solemn assembly.
14. "I hate your new moon festivals and your appointed feasts,
They have become a burden to Me.
I am weary of bearing them."

Under the particular circumstances, the otherwise God-ordained sacrifices, offerings, incense, assemblies, and feasts are an unendurable burden (vv. 13–14). Obviously the context must inform us why these good things are hated by God—and it does—the rulers of Israel had become like those of Sodom, the people like those of Gomorrah (v. 10). Their hands were "covered with blood" (v. 15). In short, at that time Israel was a

sinful nation,
[A] people weighed down with iniquity,
Offspring of evildoers,
Sons who act corruptly! (v. 4).

3. Reynolds's particular illustration is destructive of his argument. A reading of Genesis 19 will indicate the limited nature of the prohibition to look upon Sodom and Gomorrah. *Lot and his family* were forbidden to look back (v. 17) *while* God's wrath was being poured out upon the cities. Lot's wife looked back at that moment, and she died (v. 26). But Abraham looked down upon the cities shortly after the judgment and lived (vv. 27–28). Likewise, it is the long-lingering alcoholic (Prov. 23:30), one who refuses moderation (v. 35), who is forbidden to look upon the wine.

4. Although Reynolds may be correct in asserting that the reference to "red" in Proverbs 23:31 indicates the wine's alco-

holic content, it is simply not true that "there was no other word in the ancient languages in which the Bible was written for alcoholic beverages."[87] He admits to differing with the consensus of Bible translations over such a point.[88] It was shown earlier that lexicographers affirm what Reynolds denies.[89] And if he is correct in his assertion, then this one verse becomes the only verse in Scripture that warns of alcohol abuse!

Isaiah 5:21–22

> Woe to those who are wise in their own eyes,
> And clever in their own sight!
> Woe to those who are heroes in drinking wine,
> And valiant men in mixing strong drink.

This passage calls down woes upon "heroes in drinking wine." It is abundantly clear that this reference is to an immoderate abuse of wine by judges (v. 23). J. A. Alexander has noted that "the tone of this verse is sarcastic, from its using terms which express not only strength but courage and heroic spirit, in application to exploits of drunkenness."[90]

Jeremiah 35:6

> But they said, "We will not drink wine, for Jonadab, the son of Rechab, our father, commanded us, saying, 'You shall not drink wine, you or your sons, forever.' "

That this is not a universal, divine obligation to abstinence is obvious in that first, it is a human command, given by Jonadab to his sons (vv. 5, 6, 8). Second, it also forbids the owning of a house (vv. 7, 9). Third, the context of this command seems

---

87. *Ibid.*, p. 12.
88. *Ibid.*, p. 14. Here he even notes (correctly, even if irrelevantly) that "God has never provided that translators should be inerrant."
89. See pages 29ff. *supra.*
90. J. A. Alexander, *The Prophecies of Isaiah* (Grand Rapids: Zondervan, rep. 1977), I:139. See also: E. H. Plumptre, *Isaiah*, in C. J. Ellicott, *Ellicott's Commentary on the Whole Bible* (Grand Rapids: Zondervan, n.d.), IV:431; Franz Delitzsch, *Isaiah*, in Keil and Delitzsch, *Commentary*, I:178.

to imply that this was a form of prophetic theater. That is, just as Hosea was commanded to marry a harlot (Hos. 1:2; 3:1) as a symbolic portrayal of God's love for idolatrous Israel (Hos. 1:2, 4–11), so these sons were to portray a spiritual truth by keeping this vow. By being obedient to this obviously unreasonable command of their father, they would be a testimony against faithless Israel for its refusal to be obedient to God's good and reasonable law (Jer. 35:12–19).

Conclusions

The foregoing evidence has been surveyed in order to present a balanced approach to the many scriptural statements expressly dealing with alcoholic beverages. As a "people of the Book," Christians must be concerned to lay aside all preconceptions and carefully consider the express teachings of the Bible on this issue as well as others. As pointed out in the introductory chapters, the starting point and guiding standard of Christian theistic ethics is the self-validating and authoritative Word of God. The Scripture must be the believer's final arbiter in moral discourse rather than emotional, pragmatic, cultural, or intuitive considerations (although these do have some lesser place in the consideration of moral issues).

It has been so far noted that drunkenness and alcohol abuse are grave sins that lead to social, moral, and economic degradation and are expressly condemned by the Word of God. Yet it would be a hasty generalization to move from a scriptural condemnation of alcohol *abuse* to conclude that *all* drinking of alcohol is evil. This is especially true in light of the present chapter.

Here it was observed that fermented wines of all sorts played a significant role in the lives of God's people in both Old and New Testament times. In support of mandatory total abstinence, prohibitionist Henry Morris has argued that "it is significant that nowhere does the Bible actually endorse the drinking of wine or other intoxicating drinks."[91] This statement is patently false and demonstrates the all-too-frequent tendency among Christians merely to lightly review the scriptural data and proceed on intuitive feelings. *Yayin* ("wine"), which Morris himself concedes to be a fermented beverage[92], is a gift exchanged between righteous men in godly circumstances. It was an offering required by God, is expressly shown to be a blessing of God, was even symbolic of messianic blessings, and its removal was an aspect of covenantal curse. Furthermore, even our Lord Jesus Christ drank wine, produced it through miraculous intervention, and instituted the Lord's Supper with wine.

Thus, as Heinrich Seeseman has noted, "wine is very significant in Palestine," and in the Old Testament "abstinence from wine . . . is rare." Although mandatory total abstinence was not enjoined, still "there are many warnings against overindulgence."[93]

It cannot be argued that wine—*any* kind of wine, whether new wine, sweet wine, or aged strong drink—is universally prohibited in Scripture. Wine, to be sure, can be and is abused, just as other good gifts from God can be and are abused—e.g., sex (Rom. 13:13), food (Prov. 23:20–21), and wealth (1 Tim. 6:9–11). Yet sex (Heb. 13:4), food (Ps. 104:14–15), and wealth (Job 42:10–17) are meant to be good blessings and are to be used in faith and according to the directives of biblical law.

91. Henry M. Morris, *The Bible Has The Answer* (Nutley, NJ: The Craig Press, 1971), p. 162.

92. *Ibid.*

93. Seeseman, "Oinos," in Kittel, *TDNT,* V:162.

3

Bible Teaching on Christian Liberty

As was shown in chapter one, drunkenness is a heinous sin in the sight of God, but it was also demonstrated that alcoholic beverages are not merely "condoned" in Scripture. Rather, they are expressly allowed of God's people, contrary to prohibitionist arguments to the contrary. The question that arises at this juncture is this: In light of the *present* danger of alcohol abuse, should the Christian be obligated on the basis of prudence to abstain permanently from alcoholic beverages for the sake of others? This argument is what distinguishes the abstentionist position from the prohibitionist one. The difference is one of "love" versus "law"—love for those around us whom we might lead astray versus a specific biblical prohibition. It is the difference between *voluntary* total abstinence and *mandatory* total abstinence.

This is no merely academic question. It is a matter of far-reaching practical and theological importance. Is the Christian under obligation to alter his or her behavior (which in itself is not sinful) for the sake of others? And if so, to what degree, for how long, and under what circumstances? Fortunately, this very issue is addressed in detail in two forceful passages of the New Testament: Romans 14 and 1 Corinthians 8–10.

Introduction to the Analysis of Romans 14

In this part of the study greater attention will be given to the Romans 14 passage, for several reasons:

1. To study both would require far more space and time than
is presently available. The Romans 14 passage is the shorter and
more concise of the two.

2. The two passages are similar enough in their major principles and thrust that such a combined study would be both
lengthy and redundant. Specific references to particularly important statements in 1 Corinthians can easily be incorporated
into the Romans 14 exposition.

3. Romans 14, unlike the 1 Corinthians passage, makes particular and explicit reference to the exact issue at hand: wine
drinking (Rom. 14:17, 21). It is even considered by some to be
the *locus classicus* on the issue.[1]

4. First Corinthians 8 through 10, unlike the Romans 14 passage, introduces the matter from a significantly different angle.
In the 1 Corinthians material Paul deals with the issue of abstinence from foods that have been offered to idols. This is not
much of a problem for American Christians.

It should be borne in mind that Paul was writing to correct
a real, down-to-earth church problem. He does so with apostolic
wisdom insured by divine inspiration. Romans 14 is neither ab-
stract theory nor "cold" systematic theology. The church at
Rome had specific, identifiable, real-life problems involving religious scruples and their resultant discord. Sanday observes that
three specific issues seemed to be plaguing the church and that
Paul spoke to these:

> There appears to have been a party in the Church at Rome
> which had adopted certain ascetic practices over and above the
> common rule of Christianity. We gather that they abstained al-
> together from flesh and wine, and that they . . . made a point
> of observing certain days with peculiar sanctity.[2]

Furthermore, the broader context of this section of Romans
should be understood. In Romans 14 Paul seems to be explicat-

1. E.g., W. Sanday, *Romans*, in Ellicott, *Commentary*, VII:258.
2. *Ibid.*

ing two general biblical principles. First, Romans 14 gives practical expression to the command to "prove what the will of God is" in terms of Christians' differing capacities (Rom. 12:1–6). Second, in so doing it gives a direction to the application of agapic love, which is the summary of the holy law of God (Rom. 13:8–10). Thus, the passage is explaining how, in light of the obvious problems at Rome, to "put on the Lord Jesus Christ, and make no provision for the flesh in regard to its lusts" (Rom. 13:14). The following three sections will provide a verse-by-verse exposition of this important passage.

The Matter of "Weak" and "Strong" Believers: Romans 14:1–12

> *Verse 1:* Now accept the one who is weak in faith, but not for the purpose of passing judgment on his opinions.

By employment of the imperative mood, Paul *commands* the strong believer to "accept the one who is weak in faith." Although there are some similarities between the material of Romans 14 (cf. especially vv. 2–3, 6) and that of Galatians 4:10ff and Colossians 2:16–17, 20–23, there is a very basic difference as well. In Galatia and Colossae the problem over foods and days was heretical, affecting the Christian gospel at its heart, and was thus worthy of severe apostolic rebuke (cf. Gal. 1:6–9; 3:3; 4:11, 20; 5:4; and Col. 2:1–8, 14–23). In Romans the problem is one of spiritual weakness, rather than one involving a theological distortion of the truth—a distortion that would in essence incorporate alien doctrine into the very foundation of Christian soteriology.

The word employed by Paul to designate one party as "weak" is the Greek word *astheneō*. This word literally has reference to a physical ailment. The Arndt-Gingrich lexicon notes that it is used here figuratively of religious and moral weakness—the "weak" were "over-scrupulous."[3] This weakness is not left un-

3. Arndt-Gingrich, p. 115.

specified but is classified by the dative of the realm: *pistei*, "faith."
The realm of the particular weakness, then, is the realm of *faith*.
Thayer notes that Romans 14:1 (and 1 Cor. 8:9) is so con-
structed as to indicate that these weak ones were "doubtful about
things lawful and unlawful to a Christian." The term *weak* de-
scribes one "who is weak (in his feelings and conviction about
things lawful)."[4] It is important to note that Paul separates the
two groups to be dealt with in this discussion into the categories
of "weak" and "strong" in terms of their faith. Paul himself is in
the camp of the "strong" (Rom. 15:1).

The strong are urged to "receive" the weak. The customary
word used for "receive" in the Greek is *lambanō*. Here, however,
we find *proslambanō*. By the addition of the preposition *pros* to
the verb stem, Paul expresses strong emphasis,[5] as if to say: "You
must truly and fully receive the weak into your fellowship!" The
openness of their reception is further seen in that the strong are
not to receive them "for the purpose of passing judgments" on
their (weak) "opinions." That is, they are not to be received so
as to allow opportunity to corner them with the intention of
criticizing their weakness on these matters (foods, days, and
wine).[6]

> Verse 2: One man has faith that he may eat all things, but he
> who is weak eats vegetables only.

The first area of religious scrupulosity that Paul addresses is here
specified. The one who cannot eat meat is the weak one in the
context. The strong ones understand that God allows the eating
of "all things."

> Verse 3: Let not him who eats regard with contempt him who
> does not eat, and let not him who does not eat judge him who
> eats, for God has accepted him.

4. Thayer, p. 80.
5. H. E. Dana and Julius R. Mantey, *A Manual Grammar of the Greek New Testament*
(Toronto: MacMillan, 1955), p. 98: "A very frequent use of prepositions is in compo-
sition with words for the purpose of expressing emphasis or intensity."
6. Sanday, *Romans*, in Ellicott, *Commentary*, VII:258. See also: John Murray, *The
Epistle to the Romans* (Grand Rapids: Eerdmans, 1965), II:175.

Here Paul enjoins both parties with the command to mutual concern. The strong are not to "despise, disdain,"[7] "to make of no account,"[8] the one who abstains from certain foods (i.e., meat). But here Paul commands the weak to express agapic love also: the weak brother is not to "censoriously judge,"[9] or "criticize, find fault with,"[10] the strong. If the weak one does so, he is censoring one who is fully accepted by God in the matter. Murray makes a pertinent comment on this verse: "it is iniquity for us to condemn what God approves. By so doing we presume to be holier than God."[11]

> Verse 4: Who are you to judge the servant of another? To his own master he stands or falls, and stand he will, for the Lord is able to make him stand.

This continues the command to the weak relative to their treatment of the strong.[12] Basically Paul is here noting "the impropriety of intermeddling in the domestic affairs of other people."[13] Obviously, the strength of the strong (i.e., the knowledge that God allows the eating of meat) is good. It would not be improper for anyone to rebuke *sin* in a fellow Christian. The Scripture frequently exhorts believers to confront sin in the lives of others (Matt. 18:15ff; 1 Cor. 5:1–5; Gal. 6:1).

Sanday notes that "the Apostle indignantly challenges his [the weak Christian's] right to judge. That right belongs to another tribunal, before which the conduct of the stronger Christian will not be condemned but approved and upheld."[14] Thus

---

7. Arndt-Gingrich, p. 277.

8. Thayer, p. 225.

9. Murray, *Romans*, II:176. See also: Robert Jamieson, A. R. Fausett, and David Brown, *A Commentary, Critical and Explanatory on the Old and New Testaments* (Hartford: S. S. Scranton, n.d.), p. 255.

10. Arndt-Gingrich, p. 453.

11. Murray, *Romans*, II:176.

12. That Paul has not shifted his focus from the weak to the strong between verses 3 and 4 should be obvious. Cf. Murray, *Romans*, II:176; Sanday, *Romans*, in Ellicott, *Commentary*, VII:259.

13. Murray, *Romans*, II:176.

14. Sanday, *Romans*, in Ellicott, *Commentary*, VII:259.

Paul begins at this point to establish what the Westminster Confession of Faith terms the doctrine of "Christian liberty" (cf. WCF 20). No *man* can bind the conscience of another on an issue that is not condemned by Scripture either expressly or implicitly. It is significant that Paul gives directives to *both* the weak and the strong—and not just the strong, as some today seem to expect. Lenski has observed in this regard that "the weak often do more harm in the church than the strong."[15]

> *Verse 5:* One man regards one day above another, another regards every day alike. Let each man be fully convinced in his own mind.

Paul here begins addressing another source of actual contention in the church at Rome: religious observance of various holy days. He recognizes that some at Rome are convinced that the Lord has specified numerous religious days to be observed with special devotion. Paul obviously sides with the one who does *not* observe various days.[16] *If* it were the case that God still intended that the various religious holy days and festivals of the Old Testament era[17] be observed, then to fail to observe them would be disobedience to a direct command of God. This would not be a matter of "weakness" or "strength"; it would not be a matter of Christian liberty. It would be a willful sin and therefore subject to both divine and ecclesiastical censure in that "sin is lawlessness" (1 John 3:4). Paul would never leave an issue such as that to one's individual discretion. Paul is urging individual responsibility to live up to one's convictions (v. 23).

15. R.C.H. Lenski, *The Interpretation of St. Paul's Epistle to the Romans* (Minneapolis: Augsburg, 1961), p. 818.

16. Murray, *Romans*, II:178; Lenski, *Romans*, p. 821.

17. That Paul is *not* here referring to the weekly recurring sabbath should be evident based on the analogy of Scripture. Note: (1) The sabbath was a creational ordinance of perpetual obligation, Gen. 2:1–2; (2) the sabbath is one of the ten fundamental laws in the Decalogue, Exod. 20:11ff.; (3) Paul observed the sabbath, 1 Cor. 16:1–2; Acts 20:7 (in its NT form); (4) there is a similarity between this passage and those of Gal. 4:10 and Col. 2:16–17, which obviously refer to the ceremonial festal days of Old-Covenant Israel.

> *Verses 6 through 12:* He who observes the day, observes it for the Lord, and he who eats, does so for the Lord, for he gives thanks to God; and he who eats not, for the Lord he does not eat, and gives thanks to God. For not one of us lives for himself, and not one dies for himself; for if we live, we live for the Lord, or if we die, we die for the Lord; therefore whether we live or die, we are the Lord's. For to this end Christ died and lived again, that He might be Lord both of the dead and of the living. But you, why do you judge your brother? Or you again, why do you regard your brother with contempt? For we shall all stand before the judgment seat of God. For it is written, "AS I LIVE, SAYS THE LORD, EVERY KNEE SHALL BOW TO ME, AND EVERY TONGUE SHALL GIVE PRAISE TO GOD."

At this point Paul again emphasizes that there is but *one* Lord who judges a man's conscience, and each person is individually obligated only to *God's* will in terms of basic convictions. The Christian's obligation is not to the will of those about him but to the Lord who is the Judge of all men.

The Nature of the "Stumbling Block": Romans 14:13

The fact of a "stumbling block" is widely known among Christians. Unfortunately, the actual nature of this concept is not as widely known and understood. At this juncture attention will be turned to an analytical exposition of the biblical data relative to the stumbling block.

> *Verse 13:* Therefore let us not judge one another anymore, but rather determine this—not to put an obstacle or a stumbling block in a brother's way.

This is a most crucial verse in the whole discussion of Christian liberty. Based on the mutual obligations of Christians to one another, Paul here shifts his focus from a discussion of internal heartfelt attitudes and publicly expressed verbalizations (as discussed in verses 1 through 12) to a consideration of actual overt behavior that arises out of those attitudes and verbalizations.

It should be noted that Paul is beginning to address the *strong* in this passage. Note the following observations in this regard that are demonstrative of this fact:

1. He speaks in the first person in this address in verse 13: "let *us* not judge." Paul is of the camp of the strong (Rom. 15:1).

2. It would seem more logical to assume that the weak were the ones more in danger of "stumbling" by the very nature of their being weak.

3. The stumbling-block dangers have to do with convictions against the eating of certain foods (vv. 14, 21, 23). The strong do not have such scruples.

4. The stumbling results in destruction (v. 15), which suggests better the fragility of the weak.

Of utmost importance to the present issue is an explication of what Paul means when he exhorts the strong "not to put an obstacle or a stumbling block in a brother's way." To properly understand this exhortation requires a brief word study of the Greek words employed here: *proskamma* ("stumbling block") and *skandalon* ("obstacle"). As has been observed in the authoritative *Theological Dictionary of the New Testament* (hereinafter abbreviated *TDNT*):

> In Paul's pastoral handling of the debate between the strong and the weak in Corinth . . . and Rome . . . the words *skandolon, skandolizomai* [the verbal form of the former noun], *proskomma, proskoptō* [the verbal form of the preceding noun] . . . are the crucial catchwords.[18]

proskomma

In popular discussion of this important Romans 14 passage, the concept of obstacle or stumbling block is all too often obscured. Many assume it to refer to that which can perturb, disquiet, or annoy a fellow believer. However, *proskomma* has far stronger connotations than these words suggest.

18. Gustav Stahlin, "skandolon," in Gerhard Friedrich, *Theological Dictionary of the New Testament* (Grand Rapids: Eerdmans, 1971), VII:355.

In the Greek version of the Hebrew Old Testament (the Septuagint), *proskomma* occurs quite frequently. In Exodus 23:33, for instance, Israel was warned that serving false gods would be a "snare" (*proskomma*) to them. Thus, *proskomma* was that which led directly into a great sin. In Isaiah 8:14–15 Israel is warned that their rejection of Christ (who was intended to be a sanctuary for them) would cause him to become in effect their "stone of stumbling." As the cause of their stumbling, Christ would cause them to "fall and be broken," i.e., to be brought to utter ruin. Our theology would inform us that those who "stumble" (*proskoptō*) at Christ are brought to devastating and utter ruin. Consequently, *TDNT* comments on the serious consequences of *proskomma* as an obstacle by noting that "it is thus easy to see how *proskomma* . . . can be used in the sense of 'personified destruction'. . . ."[19]

In the New Testament Jesus is explicitly designated as Israel's "stone of stumbling" by reference to Isaiah 8:14 in Romans 9:32; 1 Peter 2:8; and 1 Corinthians 1:23. The prophetic utterances concerning Israel's apostasy and ruin from the lips of the Lord himself are testimony to the gravity of "stumbling" over him (e.g., Matt. 8:12; 21:43–44; 23:32–24:2). Israel's rejection of the "chief corner stone" will result in their being broken to pieces and scattered like dust (Luke 20:17–18). There is an *inseparable* connection between Israel's "stumbling" and their subsequent destruction.

Thus, Thayer's lexicon defines *proskomma* as follows: "*stumbling block*, i.e. an obstacle in the way which if one strike his foot against he necessarily stumbles or falls . . . i.e. by which it [the soul] is impelled to sin. . . ." Consequently, "to put a stumbling-block in one's way" is "to furnish one an occasion for sinning."[20] *TDNT* notes that in Romans 14 and 1 Corinthians 8 it is a "hindrance to faith" in that it is a "cause of spiritual ruin."[21] Thus, "at issue in the question of *proskomma* are ultimate decisions, conscience and faith, sin and perdition."[22]

19. Stahlin, "proskomma," in *TDNT* (1968), VI:749.
20. Thayer, p. 547.
21. Stahlin, "proskomma," in Friedrich, *TDNT*, VI:749.
22. *Ibid.*, VI:753.

skandolon

This noun and its verbal form occur frequently in the Septuagint. *TDNT* notes that in the Septuagint its "main OT mean-
ings" are "occasion of guilt" and "cause of destruction."[23] Very
simply it means "cause of ruin."[24]

In the New Testament *skandalon* is a frequently recurring word.
The Arndt-Gingrich lexicon defines it as follows: "1. *trap.*
. . . 2. *temptation to sin, enticement* to apostasy, false belief, etc."[25]
Thayer adds: "a. prop[erly], the *moveable stick* or *tricker . . . of
a trap, trap-stick. . . .* b. meta-[phorically] *any person* or *thing by
which one is* ('entrapped') *drawn into error or sin.*"[26] Thus, "as in
the OT it is the cause of both transgression and destruction."[27]
The notion that the *skandalon* is the causal factor of actual
transgression is vital to this word. Consequently, "*ta skandala* are
those who seduce into breaking the Law [in the Septuagint
usage]. In the NT interpretation they are those who lead into
sin and apostasy."[28]

In summary, when Paul enjoins the strong to a concern for
the weak, he encourages them to be careful that they not entice
or tempt a weak believer into *overtly sinful behavior.* He is *not*
teaching in this verse that Christians must avoid perturbing
other Christians. The words employed here are much too strong
for such a light employment.

The Conduct of Christian Liberty: Romans 14:14–23

Paul now begins closing in on the actual conduct of Christian
liberty in light of the fact of the presence of the weak and strong
brethren and the nature of the stumbling block.

> *Verse 14:* I know and am convinced in the Lord Jesus that
> nothing is unclean in itself; but to him who thinks anything to
> be unclean, to him it is unclean.

23. Stahlin, "skandalon," *ibid.*, VII:353.
24. *Ibid.*, p. 341.
25. Arndt-Gingrich, p. 760.
26. Thayer, p. 577.
27. Stahlin, "skandalon," in Friedrich, *TDNT,* VII:345.
28. *Ibid.*, p. 346.

Very emphatically Paul sides with the strong over against the weak concerning the eating of all foods (cf. v. 2). When Paul claims "I know and am convinced" he is speaking with clear, apostolic conviction. He is not saying "Personally, it is my opinion in this case that probably. . . ." He is convinced. Furthermore, he insists that his conviction in this matter is derived from the *Lord*—not society, not man. He will allow no debate on this principle; it is not a culturally relative ethical standard. He is convinced "in the Lord Jesus."

The apostle affirms that "nothing is unclean in itself." Murray well sums up the intent of Paul's statement in this regard:

> This principle is the refutation of all prohibitionism which lays the responsibility for wrong at the door of things rather than at man's heart. The basic evil of this ethic is that it makes God the Creator responsible and involves both blasphemy and the attempt to alleviate human responsibility for wrong.[29]

Paul's convictions are in keeping with a biblical world-view, which sees the creation as good and sin as a moral factor stirring in the irresponsible and hateful will of man. He rejects Platonic, neo-Platonic, and Gnostic conceptions of sin as an element lodged in the material realm.

While on this matter, it should be noted that some prohibitionists attempt to sidestep the issue by averring that wine is a creation not of God, but of man. Reynolds is a case in point: "Fermented beverages would not occur without man's entering into the process. (Man must press the grapes before the yeast turns the grape sugar into alcohol.)"[30] Again there arises the uneasy feeling that evidence is being virtually created *ex nihilo* in order to "prove" a point. There are many problems with observations of this nature.

In the first place, the statement is not scientifically accurate. The authoritative *Encyclopedia of Alcoholism* notes that "fermen-

29. Murray, *Romans,* II:188–189.
30. Reynolds, p. 30.

tation can occur naturally, with airborne yeasts converting any sugary mash into ethyl alcohol and carbon dioxide."[31] Even abstentionist documents have noted this, as may be seen in the Reformed Presbyterian Church, Evangelical Synod, alcohol study:

> The process of fermentation is a splitting up of sugar molecules by the action of yeast. The yeast cells are common in nature, and fermentation takes place automatically if conditions are right.[32]

The "accidental" fermentation of grape juice might be the reason behind Noah's possibly unplanned drunkenness in Genesis 9. (It may be that pre-flood atmospheric conditions prohibited fermentation processes. But after the scientifically postulated "water vapor canopy" of the early earth collapsed as a major element of the flood judgment, it was then possible for fermentation to take place, unbeknownst to Noah.) The question that naturally arises is: Should men have never begun extracting grape juice because of its natural capacity to ferment? It also needs to be noted that the text before us includes wine in its discussion of a food that is in itself a "good thing" (Rom. 14:16, 20). Finally, what becomes in such a case of Paul's statement here that "nothing is unclean of itself"? And of Jesus' teaching in Mark 7:14–23 along these lines?

Turning once again to the exposition of the text originally before us, it is true that the eating of perfectly good food can be sinful—given the proper moral context. If a man is convinced in his heart that to partake of certain foods is sinful in the sight of God (as Seventh-Day Adventists believe about pork), then for him to willfully partake of such *in light of his basic convictions urging against it*—for *him*—it is sin. If he deeply believes within his heart that eating a certain item is wrong and is forbidden by God, and yet he then partakes of that item despite his spiritual-moral convictions, he is in willful rebellion against God (cf. vv. 20, 23).

31. O'Brien-Chafetz, p. ix.
32. Gilchrist, pp. 31–32.

Verse 15: For if because of food your brother is hurt, you are no longer walking according to love. Do not destroy with your food him for whom Christ died.

How is it that the strong one's eating of food "hurt" the brother? What is Paul actually warning against here?

The Arndt-Gingrich lexicon defines the verb *lupeō* (in the verbal form found here) as follows: *"be sad, be distressed, grieve"* or *"injure, damage."*[33] The idea of "distress" or "injury" would fit best here due to the preceding context in verse 13 (see commentary above). Also, the effect of the eating by the strong is later called a "tearing down" (v. 20). The following context is thus confirmatory of the serious nature of this "hurt" (cf. especially vv. 20–23). The "hurt" is not simply annoyance, perturbance, or disappointment aroused in the weak. Murray again offers excellent commentary on Paul's train of thought:

> The grief befalling the weak is morally and religiously destructive. The sin committed, therefore, is of a grievous character and the grief can be nothing less than the vexation of conscience that afflicts a believer when he violates conscience and does what he esteems to be disloyalty to Christ.[34]

The "hurt" is the pang of a guilty conscience that results from the weak Christian's being enticed into sin (or what he *esteems* to be sin) by the behavior of the strong. The strong believer, having caused the weak to sin against his conscience, has not walked "according to love."

Verse 15 is so structured as to perhaps suggest at least the remnants of a *parallelismus membrorum* as was common in Hebraic literature. The parallelism in this case has affinities with a distich line composing a synonymous parallelism pattern. Note how the essential concepts of two parts of the thought "rhyme" in their meaning:

33. Arndt-Gingrich, p. 483.
34. Murray, *Romans*, pp. 190–191.

(a) Because of your food . . . your brother . . . is hurt.

(b) With your food . . . the one for whom Christ died . . . do not destroy.

Whether or not the above pattern is a remnant of a formal Hebraic parallelism as suggested, it should be readily apparent that the words "hurt" (*lupeō*) and "destroy" (*appollumi*) help to mutually explain each other.[35] Consequently, the hurt caused in the weak believer is equivalent to his being destroyed.

Appollumi is a very strong word that means to "ruin, destroy,"[36] "to put out of the way entirely, abolish, put an end to, ruin . . . render useless."[37] Speaking of the specific verse under consideration, lexicographers and commentators are generally agreed that it means "by one's conduct to cause another to lose eternal salvation."[38] Presbyterian theologian Charles Hodge noted in a comment on this verse that:

> Believers (the elect) are constantly spoken of as in danger of perdition. They are saved only if they continue steadfast unto the end. If they apostatize, they perish. If the Scriptures tell the people of God what is the tendency of their sins, as to themselves, they may tell them what is the tendency of such sins as to others.[39]

Simply put, Paul is here warning that the logical outcome of enticing the weaker brother into sinning against his conscience

---

35. This can be insisted upon apart from the conjecture that there exists in the structure of this verse a *parallelismus membrorum* on the following grounds: (1) The obvious close relation of v. 15a with v. 15c., regardless of a lack of formal structure; (2) The preceding context as discussed above suggests the stronger meaning of the verb *lupeō*; (3) The following context which indicates the weaker Christian is "torn down," v. 20. To be "sad" is not equivalent to being "torn down."

36. Arndt-Gingrich, p. 94.

37. Thayer, p. 64.

38 *Ibid.*, p. 64. See also Arndt-Gingrich, p. 94.

39. Charles Hodge, *Commentary on the Epistle to the Romans* (Grand Rapids: Eerdmans, 1886, rep. 1972), p. 424. See also: Robert L. Dabney, *Lectures in Systematic Theology* (Grand Rapids: Zondervan, 1878, rep. 1972), pp. 697ff. Louis Berkhof, *Systematic Theology* (Grand Rapids: Eerdmans, 1941, rep. 1972), p. 397. A. A. Hodge, *Outlines of Theology* (Edinburgh: Banner of Truth, 1860, rep. 1972), pp. 544ff.

is the utter loss of his salvation and his resultant final perdition. Although no true believer can, in fact, lose his unmerited, sovereignly bestowed salvation, Paul's language here is in keeping with numerous biblical warnings against apostasy in just such terms. It, then, is a very serious matter that the strong not behave in such a way as to actually lead the weaker Christian into sinning against his conscience, which entails his utter grief and destruction.

> *Verses 16 and 17:* Therefore do not let what is for you a good thing be spoken of as evil; for the kingdom of God is not eating and drinking, but righteousness and peace and joy in the Holy Spirit.

The "therefore" draws a conclusion to what Paul has just stated in verses 13 through 15 concerning the conduct of the strong. The "good thing" refers to the strong one's sure knowledge of Christian liberty. Paul's exhortation here is this: Because there are weaker believers who feel it wrong to eat or drink certain things—and because the strong can tempt them to sin against the dictates of their conscience—therefore the strong must not abuse his liberty to the degree that he does lead weaker believers to sin against their consciences. If he does so, his Christian liberty will be the subject of ridicule and scorn.

> *Verses 18 and 19:* For he who in this way serves Christ is acceptable to God and approved by men. So then let us pursue the things which make for peace and the building up of one another.

Paul teaches that the strong who use their liberty wisely, carefully, and lovingly not only please God but will find approval in the sight of men. Before, the abuser of liberty was the cause of scorn and ridicule among men because of his enticing weaker believers into sin against their consciences (v. 16). The two effects are opposites: the abuser receives ridicule; the wise user of Christian liberty is approved by men. Consequently, it is appropriate for the strong to actively seek peace and edification among all believers.

The particular problems of this church should be recalled in order to gain the proper perspective on this statement. From verses 1, 3, 4, 10, and 13 it is obvious that the two camps—the strong and the weak—were warring over religious scruples. Rather than edifying each other, they were passing judgment, disapproving, and holding each other up to ridicule and contempt.

> *Verse 20:* Do not tear down the work of God for the sake of food. All things indeed are clean, but they are evil for the man who eats and gives offense.

Since the primary concern of the kingdom of God is not eating and drinking, but essential spiritual qualities that govern eating and drinking (v. 17), the strong one should not abuse his Christian liberty. If he is causing weak believers to stumble into sin (v. 13) and be deeply grieved for their rebellion (v. 15a)—which if logically dwelled in was equivalent to apostasy (v. 15c)—then the strong one was tearing down the "work of God," the weak believer.

". . . they are evil for the man who eats and gives offense" (v. 20c) teaches that when the weaker brother is finally lured into eating against his conscience, he "offends" (*proskomatta*)—he sins against his own conscience and thus against what he believes to be the will of God.

> *Verse 21:* It is good not to eat meat or to drink wine or to do anything by which your brother stumbles.

Before considering the exegesis of this verse, a textual comment needs to be made. The Authorized Version (KJV) adds to this verse the following words: ". . . or is offended, or is made weak." The better Greek manuscripts compel us to leave these words out. Eminent Greek scholar Bruce M. Metzger, in his important *A Textual Commentary on the Greek New Testament*, suggests that these additional words, which occur in a few ancient manuscripts, were a later copyist's expansion of the text.[40] In keeping with this evidence, the United Bible Societies' third edition of *The Greek New Testament* omits the words from the text and relegates them to a footnote, thus indicating their dubious authenticity. The twenty-third edition of Nestle's *Novum Testamentum Graece* does so also. The R.V.G. Tasker *Greek New Testament* omits them without so much as a comment. Versions that follow suit include the New American Standard Bible, American Standard Version, New International Version, Revised Standard Version, Phillips, New English Bible, and Today's English Version. Thus, we will not consider them as authentic to the original text.

Perhaps, with Romans 14:13 and 1 Corinthians 8:13, this verse has been one of the more misunderstood verses in the context of the debate over Christian liberty. Some would wrongly understand this verse to mean that all Christians everywhere and under all circumstances are obligated by Holy Writ to maintain a life of total abstinence. That this is patently false can easily be seen by a quick reading of the text. Do the same people insist upon total abstinence from *meat* based on the text? Paul does say, "It is good not to eat meat or drink wine. . . ."

Others who call for total abstinence argue in the following manner: "In light of the abuse of alcohol in present American culture the Christian should abstain from alcoholic beverages. After all, meat is *not* abused in America." This argument, of course, overlooks the ridicule in vogue by the socialist world-planners, who claim that if America would quit feeding its grain to beef cattle, the whole world would have more bread. Those of this school of thought claim that America's love for grain-fed beef causes millions to starve to death by reducing the world's grain supply.[41] First Corinthians 8:13 is often brought in to sup-

---

40. Bruce Manning Metzger, *A Textual Commentary on the Greek New Testament* (London: United Bible Societies, p. 1971), p. 532.

41. See: Ron Sider, *Rich Christians in an Age of Hunger* (Downer's Grove, IL: InterVarsity Press, 1977), pp. 25, 42–44. Also see Lester R. Brown, *In the Human Interest* (New York: Norton, 1974); C. Dean Freudenberger and Paul M. Minus, Jr., *Christian Responses in a Hungry World* (Nashville: Abingdon, 1976); Kenneth Cauthen, *Christian Biopolitics* (Nashville: Abingdon, 1971), pp. 35ff.

plement the exposition of this verse. It reads: "Therefore, if food causes my brother to stumble, I will never eat meat again, that I might not cause my brother to stumble."

Several observations will help put this class of verses on Christian liberty into a proper perspective:

First, it is quite obvious that Paul puts the religiously scrupled abstainers in the category of the "weak":

(a) He couples abstinence from meat and wine together. Earlier he had taught that those who abstained from meat were not strong (Rom. 14:1).

(b) The previous verses warned of the danger of the weak stumbling at the liberty of the strong. That is precisely what is being spoken of in verse 21.

(c) He is persuaded that nothing is unclean of itself (vv. 14, 20), but that the uncleanness arises in the mind of the partaker (v. 23).

Second, the admonition here is given in a specific social context: the strong is to abstain on the occasions when it would possibly lure the weaker believers to stumble (i.e., actually sin against their conscience). When Paul says it is good not "to eat" and not "to drink" he does so by employing the aorist infinitive. Blass-DeBrunner's classic work, *A Greek Grammar of the New Testament,* makes a grammatical observation on the use of the aorist infinitive in this specific instance:

> the aor[ist] is to be taken strictly: "it is good not to eat meat *for once* (in a specific instance) if it might cause offense"; it is not a question of continuous abstention.[42]

Lenski in his commentary agrees when he comments that "The aorists are to be understood exactly: eating at *one time* . . . in a given case, where offense would be caused; permanent abstinence is not discussed."[43] Jamieson, Fausset, and Brown note in their commentary that

42. F. Blass and A. DeBrunner, *A Greek Grammar of the New Testament and Other Early Christian Literature* (Chicago: University of Chicago Press, 1961), p. 174.

43. Lenski, *Romans,* p. 849.

[Paul's] directions are to be considered not as *prescriptions for one's entire lifetime,* even to promote the good of men on a large scale, but simply as cautions against the too free use of Christian liberty. . . .[44]

Clearly the prohibition against meat or wine is not a universally mandatory obligation. It is simply enjoined upon strong believers when the real possibility exists that a brother may in fact be lured into doing that which he personally deems to be evil.

Third, 1 Corinthians 8:13 must be understood in this same respect. There Paul says he would "*never* eat meat again." The following comments need to be made on this statement:

(*a*) He does not say that he was in fact going to abstain from meat because some stumble because of it. He speaks in a conditional sense: "if."

(*b*) This is not a *command* that is apostolically binding upon others. It is Paul's personal testimony as to how *he* would choose to handle a specific situation. (This is of a similar nature with his testimony in 1 Corinthians 7:7–8, where Paul suggests that it is good for the unmarried to remain unmarried "even as I.") Note the lack of imperatival exhortation and the personal reference to himself: "*I* will never eat meat again."

(*c*) All of this is conditioned by a certain circumstance: Paul will not eat meat over again *if* his eating would *cause a brother to stumble* (i.e., sin against his conscience and be destroyed). Certainly we cannot think that everywhere Paul went and in every moment of his life there were Christians crowded around him ready to stumble over this issue.

Fourth, in the broader context of Paul's teaching we find a twofold reason for any temporary abstinence from food, wine, or any sort of things:

(*a*) As listed above, he would abstain so as to not prompt a brother into sinning against his conscience.

(*b*) In 1 Corinthians 9:20–23 another aim of his temporary abstention would be to eventually rid the weaker brother of his

44. Jamieson, Fausset, and Brown, *Commentary,* II:256.

weakness, that is, to train him up in strength in that matter—
not to confirm his ill-founded religious scrupulosity and establish
him in his weakness.[45] "To the weak I became weak, [in order]
that I might win the weak . . ." (1 Cor. 9:22). The Christian
does the weaker brother no favor by encouraging him to remain
in his state of weakness. With a balanced and gentle approach
and patient teaching, the weak can become strong.

> *Verses 22 and 23:* The faith which you have, have as your own
> conviction before God. Happy is he who does not condemn him-
> self in what he approves. But he who doubts is condemned if he
> eats, because his eating is not from faith; and whatsoever is not
> from faith is sin.

Paul does not request the strong to relinquish their convictions. He could not have done so—they were proper in terms
of a biblical, godly world-view. The exhortation is to not bran-
dish one's Christian liberty unlovingly: remember that your conviction is good and should be used in a way pleasing before God.
The strong one can happily eat meat and drink wine, because
his conscience does not condemn him (and properly so) in ap-
proving what he eats and drinks.

However, if a man doubts that it is right to eat meat or drink
wine (by contextual implication) and yet still eats or drinks in
defiance of what he deems to be contrary to the will of God,
then he is condemning himself. We must always strive for a clear
conscience before God (cf. Acts 24:16; 1 Tim. 1:3–5). "What-
soever is not of faith is sin."

A Summary of Principles

The foregoing study was necessary to set up the proper biblical
understanding of the often-misunderstood doctrine of Christian

---

45. Cf. Lenski, *Romans,* p. 850. Lenski, *The Interpretation of 1 and 2 Corinthians*
(Minneapolis: Augsburg, 1961), pp. 379–380; Charles Hodge, *Commentary on the First
Epistle to the Corinthians* (Grand Rapids: Eerdmans, 1835, rep. 1969), p. 166; Jamieson,
Fausset, and Brown, *Commentary,* 2:279.

liberty. However, it was lengthy, encumbered with exegetical and theological detail, and laboriously footnoted. The following summation will concisely condense the principles implicit in Romans 14. The verse references should cue the reader not only to the biblical text, but back to the preceding commentary on the text.

1. Within the church there are Christians at all levels of growth and maturation. Some are weak in the faith (vv. 1, 2, 23; 15:1), whether due to newness in the faith (1 Peter 2:2) or to "spiritual retardation," for whatever reasons (1 Cor. 3:1–3). Yet others are strong in the faith (vv. 2, 13, 22; 15:1). This is undoubtedly the case not only in the Roman situation, but in every church throughout the course of church history.

2. The strong are obligated by apostolic command to fully accept the weak into their Christian fellowship and community (vv. 1, 3, 10; 15:1). Christianity is not elitist. We are all members of the body of Christ through his sovereign action in overcoming our sinful rebellion, not by our own wisdom, effort, or purity. Yet the weak are also under apostolic obligation to not criticize the strong for their God-approved convictions (vv. 3, 4, 10). "Affirmative action" is not a biblical ideal.

3. The Lord, and the Lord alone, is the only Lord of an individual's conscience (vv. 3, 4, 7–9, 12–13, 22). To him we stand or fall; to him must we give a final account. And the Lord has not left us to grope in darkness regarding his will for us. He has given us his word to direct us in the paths of righteousness. We must live by every word that proceeds out of the mouth of God, not man.

4. As long as we hold to something as a devout and religious conviction, we are obligated to consistency in the living out of that conviction (vv. 5, 12, 22–23). The essence of sin is living against God; and if we truly and deeply believe something to be of God, we must live in terms of that belief.

5. We are not to censoriously judge a fellow believer in adiaphora, i.e., "things indifferent" (vv. 10, 13, 19). If a particular action is not forbidden by either express command or clear prin-

ciple derived by good and necessary inference from Scripture, then we cannot judge those who engage in such actions.

6. The strong one must not abuse his Christian liberty so as to entice, prompt, or ensnare weaker Christians into sinning against their own deeply rooted convictions. That is, the stronger believer must be careful to not put the weaker believer in a position in which he will actually do what he is convinced is morally or spiritually wrong (vv. 13, 15, 16, 20–23). This would be to tempt the weaker brother into an "attitudinal sin." That is, even though the action itself is not sinful, the fact that the weaker brother *believes* it to be sinful makes it a sin for him. He would then be doing something that he felt was rebellious before God.

7. There is nothing in God's creation that is intrinsically evil. Evil is a moral condition operative in persons, whether angelic, human, or otherwise. It is not a material property somehow rooted in tangible creation (vv. 14, 20). As the Lord himself said,

> Listen to Me, all of you, and understand: there is nothing outside the man which going into him can defile him; but the things which proceed out of the man are what defile the man. . . . For from within, out of the heart of men, proceed the evil thoughts, fornications, thefts, murders, adulteries, deeds of coveting and wickedness, as well as deceit, sensuality, envy, slander, pride and foolishness. All these evil things proceed from within and defile the man [Mark 7:14–15, 21–23].

8. Love and peace should characterize Christian relations (vv. 15, 17, 19). We are all brothers in Christ, members of one body. We must therefore work together as a body to the glory of God.

9. There are certain occasions where it may be best to *temporarily* and *voluntarily* abstain from certain things (e.g., wine, meat, and so on) that are otherwise good—if there is a real danger of luring a weaker Christian into a situation in which he will act contrary to the dictates of his moral and spiritual conscience (v. 21; cf. 1 Cor. 8:13).

10. The strong should rejoice in their knowledge of God's approval (vv. 18, 22) and should gently and patiently seek to win the weak to a stronger position (cf. 15:1; 1 Cor. 9:20–23). Unfortunately, it is too often the case that the strong are expected to come around to the weaker brother's position, thereby confirming him in his weakness.

Conclusions

Christians must be careful not only to encourage the strong one to patiently forgo his privilege on just occasion, but must also exhort the weak to refrain from judging the stronger. The issue of Christian liberty involves *mutual* concern and edification. One class of believers is not to be preferred above the other.

As the present study on Christian liberty is drawn to a close, the following paragraphs by Charles Hodge and John Calvin merit close attention in this regard.

Charles Hodge has written that:

> The gospel does not make religion to consist in external observances. . . .
>
> It is a great error in morals, and a great practical evil, to make that sinful which is in fact innocent. Christian love never requires this or any other sacrifice of truth. Paul would not consent, for the sake of avoiding offence, that eating all kinds of food, even what had been offered to idols, or disregarding sacred festivals of human appointment, should be made a sin; he strenuously and openly maintained the reverse. He represents those who thought differently, as weak in faith, as being under an error, from which more knowledge and more piety would free them. . . .
>
> We should stand fast in the liberty wherewith Christ has made us free, and not allow our consciences to be brought under the yoke of bondage to human opinions. There is a strong tendency in men to treat, as matters of conscience, things which God has never enjoined. . . .
>
> It is often necessary to assert our Christian liberty at the expense of incurring censure, and offending even good men, in

order that right principles of duty may be preserved. Our Saviour consented to be regarded as a Sabbath-breaker, and even a 'wine-bibber and a friend of publicans and sinners'; but wisdom was justified of her children. [46]

Elsewhere Hodge has given the following insights into the matter:

It is morally obligatory, therefore, to abstain from indulging in things indifferent, when the use of them is the occasion of sin to others. This is a principle the application of which must be left to every man's conscience in the fear of God. No rule of conduct, founded on expediency, can be enforced by church discipline. It was right in Paul to refuse to eat flesh for fear of causing others to offend; but he could not have been justly exposed to discipline, had he seen fit to eat it. He circumcised Timothy, and refused to circumcise Titus. Whenever a thing is right or wrong according to circumstances, every man must have the right to judge of those circumstances. [47]

Calvin helps us to make a vital distinction in Christian liberty when he speaks of the difference between an "offense given" and an "offense received" (or taken):

Here, then, I shall say something about offenses—how they are to be distinguished, which ones avoided, which overlooked. From this we may afterward be able to determine what place there is for our freedom among men. Now I like that common distinction between an offense given and one received, inasmuch as it has the clear support of Scripture and properly expresses what is meant.

If you do anything with unseemly levity, or wantonness, or rashness, out of its proper order or place, so as to cause the ignorant and the simple to stumble, such will be called an offense given by you, since by your fault it came about that this sort of offense arose. And, to be sure, one speaks of an offense as given

46. Hodge, *Romans*, pp. 429–430.
47. Hodge, *1 Corinthians*, p. 151.

in some matter when its fault arises from the doer of the thing itself.

An offense is spoken of as received when something, otherwise not wickedly or unseasonably committed, is by ill will or malicious intent of mind wrenched into occasion for offense. Here is no "given" offense. . . .[48]

48. John Calvin, *Institutes of the Christian Religion* (Philadelphia: Westminster Press, 1960), I:842, 843. Found at *Institutes,* Book 3, chapter 19, section 11.

4

Concluding Statements

The thrust of this study has been designedly narrow. The intent has been to research and analyze the biblical data relative to the *general* question of the *morality* of alcohol consumption.

In the final analysis it seems abundantly clear that Scripture does not demand either universal total abstinence or prohibition. Although it is the case that alcoholic beverages can be, have been, and are presently abused by individuals, such need not be the case. Indeed, the biblical record frequently and clearly speaks of alcoholic beverages as good gifts from God to be enjoyed by man. Unfortunately, as is always the case among sinners, good things are often transformed into curses. This is true not only with alcohol but with sex, wealth, authority, and many other areas of life.

The reader should not conclude that this study represents an encouragement to drinking to those who do not presently do so. It is not. The author has never and will never encourage others to drink. Whether or not an individual wants to drink is a matter of his or her own tastes and discretion (within biblical limits, of course). Neither should it be thought that this study presents all that can be said on the whole question of alcohol. Again, such is not the case. For instance, there are various state concerns and obligations that undoubtedly justify governmental involvement in the use of alcoholic beverages, e.g., forbidding alcohol consumption for certain ages and under certain conditions, punishing abuse of alcoholic beverages, insuring reasonable health standards relative to its production, enforcing truth-in-advertising in its promotion, and so forth. These and numerous other aspects of the alcohol question need adequate consideration.

The only concern before the reader has been the consideration of the question of whether or not God allows alcohol consumption. Too often the Bible has taken the back seat in arguments pro and con. This is most unfortunate—especially when considering the matter in ecclesiastical circles. If Christians are to endeavor to reconstruct society in terms of their cultural mandate and along the lines of biblical law, they must do so out of intense reflection on the biblical data. In other words, they must "let God be found true" (Rom. 3:4).

The "Potential Alcoholic"

Often the fear is expressed that the moderationist position has dangerous implications for the "potential alcoholic." Generally this question presupposes a genetic predisposition to alcoholism. Certainly it is true that different people have different levels of tolerance to alcohol. But the notion that alcoholism is somehow a physiological defect is antithetical to the biblical doctrine of sin and of personal responsibility.[1]

The Bible clearly labels drunkenness a moral failure and a spiritual sin (Gal. 5:19–21). Chronic drunkenness is even taught to be a condition that effectively bars entrance into the kingdom of God (1 Cor. 6:9–10). Furthermore, the assertion that the imbibing of alcohol is a form of reckless conduct, in light of the many unknown "potential alcoholics," impugns the character of both the apostles and even the Lord Jesus Christ himself. Did not they partake of wine openly (e.g., Luke 7:33–35)? Were they guilty of endangering those who were "physiologically defective"? Did they leave a bad example for future Christians in this regard? Did Jesus not know of "potential alcoholics" or of "constitutional alcoholism"? In addition, what becomes of the justice of God if he bars from his kingdom the "physiological defective" (whom he has made, Exod. 4:11)? Surely it is not the case that the Lord would punish someone for a genetic fault or a physiological malformity.

---

1. Cf. Jay E. Adams, *Competent to Counsel* (Phillipsburg, NJ: Presbyterian and Reformed, 1970), p. xiv and *passim.*

Along these lines, comments by Christian ethicist and philosopher Greg L. Bahnsen may prove helpful. He is dealing with an analogous ethical situation, although not identical to alcohol use. In this case he answers arguments that homosexuality is a problem of physiological constitution or genetic predisposition.

> In a theological context it might mean that the depraved nature with which men are born is for some individuals specifically oriented to the sinful perversion of homosexuality. However, the Scripture does not support the idea that each person receives a sinful nature with a peculiar bent toward particular transgressions of God's will. Every man inherits a general depravity of heart, a fundamental disinclination to good, a pervasive misdirection, which affects every aspect of his person without discriminating emphases; there is a wholesale, general pollution operating in everything he is and does. Nevertheless, the ways in which individual sinners develop their depraved natures, the particular sins upon which they focus and around which their characters are formed, will differ from person to person.[2]

Bahnsen's comments are clearly and easily applicable to the matter under consideration.

Alcoholism researcher John Langone has written:

> Heredity, errors in the body's chemistry that prevent the alcoholic from using alcohol properly, brain defects, allergy, vitamin deficiency, glandular problems, a defective "thermostat" that causes an uncontrollable thirst for alcohol all have been examined by researchers. But thus far, none has been shown to be specifically responsible for alcoholism. There is no physical examination or blood test that can yet be performed to determine why a person has become an alcoholic, or whether he or she will become one; and no one has isolated a specific gene, that unit of heredity, for alcoholism.[3]

2. Greg L. Bahnsen, *Homosexuality: A Biblical View* (Grand Rapids: Baker, 1978), p. 69.

3. John Langonne, *Bombed, Buzzed, Smashed . . . or Sober* (Boston: Little, Brown, and Co. 1976), p. 57.

Morris Chafetz, M.D., noted authority on alcoholism with the National Institute on Alcohol and Alcohol Abuse (hereinafter: NIAAA), has even written:

> Some say that only a hairline separates the social or moderate drinker from the alcoholic. Don't you believe it—a grand canyon separates them.[4]

Now all of this is not brought forward in order to trivialize the truly serious problem of alcoholism, nor to scoff at the potential danger of alcohol for those prone to immoderate excess. There are people who have problems with alcohol—*but the problem is due to moral failure, not physiological defect.* The circumspect Christian should be aware of the sinful tendencies of acquaintances in this direction and should avoid causing such to "stumble" by tempting them to partake.

4. Morris E. Chafetz, M.D., *Liquor: The Servant of Man* (Boston: Little, Brown, and Co., 1965), p. 9.

APPENDIX **B**

Alcohol and Health

Christian theology recognizes that the body of man is a creation of God (Gen. 2:7) and that the Christian's body is the "temple of the Holy Spirit" (1 Cor. 6:19). These twin truths of creation and redemption have a direct and important bearing on the Christian's concern for health. It is often alleged that alcohol consumption *per se* is hazardous to one's health.[1] As stated in the introductory chapter, it is not the purpose of this study to explore the medical data relative to alcohol use. However, to allay the fears in this direction, two points need to be considered.

First, the teaching of Scripture implies that alcoholic beverages are not health hazards in themselves. Were this the case, then both the integrity of Scripture and the goodness of God would be called into question. It has been amply demonstrated by extensive biblical argumentation that alcoholic beverages are allowed for Christian use. For instance, it was shown in chapter two that alcoholic wine was a worthy gift between righteous men and was even deemed a blessing from God. Furthermore, it was demonstrated that Christ himself partook of it and that he even instructed that the Lord's Supper include wine. Surely all of this was not done in detriment to man's health considerations. As a matter of fact, Timothy was even exhorted to take a little wine for reasons of better health (1 Tim. 5:23).

Second, except for those with a vehement intellectual predisposition against alcoholic beverages, there are few medical au-

---

1. Reynolds, pp. 33, 55.

thorities who teach that moderate alcohol consumption is generally harmful to one's health. Indeed, quite the opposite may be true! There is an increasing wealth of data that demonstrates that alcoholic beverages are in fact generally *beneficial* to health under normal circumstances.

Morris E. Chafetz of NIAAA has an enlightening observation on the matter before us:

> Between effects of heavy or excessive alcohol intake and moderate drinking there is a great distinction. Excessive consumption increases mortality and produces various types of damage. . . . However, there is no evidence of damaging effects even from the steady intake of moderate amounts and, indeed, mortality statistics reviewed elsewhere in this *Report* suggest a possible beneficial effect.[2]
>
> [He continues by noting that:] In view of the statistical indications that moderate drinkers live longer than abstainers, it seems possible that the beneficial effect of moderate drinking may apply especially to old age.[3]

The beneficial effect of alcohol on the human body seems to be especially (though not exclusively) related to the heart, for as the NIAAA has noted: "Some epidemiological data suggest that the risk for coronary artery disease may be smaller in light drinkers than abstainers."[4]

Yet despite such evidence, Reynolds writes regarding Paul's advice to Timothy in 1 Timothy 5:23 (which relates only to the stomach): "But for Timothy's *stomach* he could never have recommended alcohol. It is known now, and was probably known

2. *Alcohol and Health: New Knowledge*, Morris E. Chafetz, M.D., Chairman, Task Force, U.S. Dept. of Health, Education and Welfare: National Institute on Alcohol Abuse and Alcoholism. *Second Special Report to the U.S. Congress on Alcohol and Health* (DHEW Pub. No. HDM-75-212), Washington, D.C.: U. S. Government Printing Office, 1974, p. 33.

3. *Ibid.* In fact, this same report also notes that "alcohol is normally present in all mammals," being produced in the intestinal tract (p. 76).

4. Information and Feature Service, National Institute on Alcohol Abuse and Alcoholism (IFS No. 53, Nov. 30, 1978), p. 4. See also Chafetz, *Alcohol and Health*, p. 72; Langonne, *Bombed* (note 3, Appendix A) p. 95.

then, that alcohol does nothing good to the stomach."[5] He then insists that Paul's prescription called for pure, unfermented grape juice. (Reynolds argues that when "wine" is spoken of in a good sense in the Bible, it cannot be alcoholic. In light of this principle of interpretation, one must wonder why the Good Samaritan poured grape juice in the wounds of the assaulted Jew in Luke 10:34!)

Contrary to both the general tendency of Reynolds's position with regard to alcohol and health and his specific comment on 1 Timothy 5:23, Raymond McCarthy, editor of *Drinking and Intoxication*, has stated:

> In moderate amounts alcohol stimulates the flow of gastric juices and promotes stomach motility. . . . There is no evidence that alcohol ever causes gastric ulcers, doctors forbid their ulcer patients to drink because of the increased gastric flow. Moderate amounts of alcohol do not interfere with digestion; they may even promote it.[6]

Of course, none of this—whether from the Bible or scientific data—denies the obvious fact that there are certain physiological abnormalities (e.g., allergies) and particular conditions (e.g., pregnancy) that may preclude the safe consumption of alcohol. This is true of not only alcohol but other substances, such as even cow's milk, penicillin, aspirin, and so on. Nevertheless, it cannot be credibly argued *in general* that alcoholic beverages are harmful to health.

5. Reynolds, p. 55.

6. Raymond McCarthy, ed., *Drinking and Intoxication* (Glencoe, IL: Free Press, 1959), p. 10.

Alcohol and the Christian Witness

It is often argued that Christians should totally abstain from alcohol as a witness to both our sinful, hedonistic culture and to our own weaker Christian brothers. Harold Lindsell has argued this point:

> When one considers these statistics [i.e., demographic studies on alcohol abuse] and ponders the numerous drawbacks to the use of alcohol, it remains for those who advocate its use to demonstrate its value and benefits. There is no argument in its favor that is not outweighed by the drawbacks. The Christian has a particular responsibility in this matter because of the significance his life style and influence have on others.[1]

Gleason Archer, conservative Old Testament scholar, agrees:

> If we really care about the souls of men, and if we are really in business for Christ rather than for ourselves, then there seems (to this writer, at least) to be no alternative to total abstinence—not as a matter of legalism, but rather as a matter of love.[2]

It is true that Christians are to be an example to others (1 Tim. 4:12; 1 Cor. 4:16; 11:1). This witness-by-example is an

---

1. Lindsell, p. 116.
2. Gleason Archer, *Encyclopedia of Bible Difficulties* (Grand Rapids: Zondervan, 1982), p. 149.

important aspect of our calling to glorify God in all of life. But, for several reasons, it does not follow that a moderate partaking of alcoholic beverages is forbidden the believer on these grounds.

First, we must again be reminded that the Lord and his apostles partook of wine despite the fact that sinful men indulged in it to their own hurt and degradation. The Bible frequently and unsparingly condemns drunkenness. As a matter of fact, "The Bible affords ample proof that excessive drinking of intoxicants was a common vice among the Hebrews, as among other ancient peoples."[3]

Second, the character of the Christian witness must be molded by biblical truth. The truth of the matter is that the Bible does not condemn moderate consumption of alcohol. The "Christian witness" argument cannot schizophrenically maintain that Christians are obligated to avoid that which Scripture allows! Our witness is detracted from, not enhanced, if we promote a false morality, a morality presumably "higher" than the Bible. The biblical witness to the world relative to alcohol should be that of moderation (cf. e.g., Acts 24:25; Gal. 5:23).

Third, even in the occasional cases where a temporary total abstinence is prudent as a matter of witness, the goal of such abstinence must be to witness against the sinfulness of the sinner's *weakness.* When Paul became "all things to all men" (e.g., when he abstained from wine in the presence of the weak), he did so with the long-range goal of demonstrating the failure of weakness and the error of the contrary position. In 1 Corinthians 9:22 he writes: "To the weak I became weak." This was not to encourage them in their weakness. It was not his adoption of a permanent lifestyle. He continues: "To the weak I became weak, *that I might win the weak.*" Paul's temporary abstinence, for example, would be designed to ultimately show the weak one his error and to win him away from his weakness, his misapprehension of biblical morality. This is not to say that the moderationist seeks to get the "weaker" brother to drink. It is simply to say

3. Edwards, "Drunkenness," *ISBE,* II:880.

that the weak brother is encouraged to see the error of his *position*, not necessarily of his *practice*.

Fourth, such a principle of conduct knows no limits and can lead to all manner of erroneous prohibitions similar to the situation of Pharisaism. It was mentioned previously that there are those who deem America's love for beef to be sinful in light of worldwide hunger. Allegedly our grain-fed beef consumes an "unfair" amount of the world's grain supply. Some would, as a matter of principle, encourage abstinence from beef as a Christian witness. Such radical (but logical) calls for abstinence could be multiplied in illustration of the "Christian witness" argument against the moderationist view. However, if one's moral guidelines are drawn from Scripture, free rein is not given to the imagination or cultural holiness.

APPENDIX **D**

The Old Testament and Watered Wine

Even some who deem wine drinking as everywhere and always evil will concede that fermented wine was actually drunk in the Bible. But they will then insist that it was always diluted with water. For a variety of reasons, this objection cannot be validly employed as an argument destructive of the moderationist position or as one demonstrative of either the abstentionist or prohibitionist positions.

First, it must be noted that *all* the evidence supportive of this contention is drawn from extrabiblical sources that are later than the Old Testament era.[1] Even granting this practice, it should be noted not only that it is a later innovation and thus irrelevant to the Old Testament law, but that the New Testament itself is wholly silent on the matter. Furthermore, none of this non-biblical data demands that the entire culture always and everywhere diluted wine for daily use.

Second, in the biblical record there is absolutely no distinguishing of "undiluted" (i.e., unsafe) wine and "diluted" (i.e., safe) wine. Were it a mark of righteousness to avoid undiluted wine and to enjoy only diluted wine, why is the Scripture silent on the matter? Is not the Scripture "profitable for teaching, for reproof, for correction, for training in righteousness; that the

1. E.g., Robert Stein, "Wine Drinking in New Testament Times" in *Christianity Today* (June 20, 1975).

man of God may be adequate, equipped for every good work"
(2 Tim. 3:16–17)?

Third, recognized biblical scholars of all schools of thought on
the use of wine in Scripture are in virtual agreement on the non-
diluted nature of wine in the Old Testament. Emmet Russell is
apparently of the abstentionist persuasion in that he writes:
"Whatever use Jesus or others made of wine is no proof that its
use in our tense age is wise. The Bible gives more space to the
danger than to the benefit of wine."[2] Yet he also categorically
states that "in OT times wine was not diluted."[3]

Burton Scott Easton agrees: "In OT times wine was drunk
undiluted, and wine mixed with water was thought to be ruined."[4]

Fourth, although there are numerous passages speaking of
"mixed wines" (some referring to different wines mixed together,
others to wines mixed with various herbs and spices), there is
only one passage where water-diluted wine is mentioned: Isaiah
1:22. It is worthy of note that this sole reference to water-diluted
wine speaks of such a practice in a negative manner: "Your silver
has become dross, / Your drink[5] diluted with water." Old Testament scholar E. J. Young comments on the "dilution" or
"weakening" of wine in this passage:

> *weakened* — Literally, "cut." By means of cutting, the strength
> of wine is impaired. *sov'ek* is fine wine, used here in parallelism
> with *kaspeck*, "thy silver." The metal that was so pure that light
> could find in it a clear reflection, as well as the fine wine of the
> land, was destroyed, the wine having been weakened (lit., cut,
> mutilated, circumcised, castrated) by water.[6]

The statement here seems to be based partly in actual fact

2. Emmet Russell, "Wine" in Merrill C. Tenney, ed., *The Zondervan Pictorial Bible
Dictionary* (Grand Rapids: Zondervan, 1967), p. 895.

3. *Ibid.*

4. Easton, "Wine," *ISBE*, IV:3087.

5. The Hebrew word for "drink" is *sobe*, which is rare. It denotes a fine wine that
can intoxicate. As a matter of fact, it is related to the word *saba* which means "drunkard," cf. Deut. 21:20; Prov. 23:21; Nah. 1:10.

6. E. J. Young, *The Book of Isaiah* (Grand Rapids: Eerdmans, 1965), I:82.

and partly in figurative allusion. That is, the city of Jerusalem, which had become a "harlot" filled with "murderers" (Isa. 1:21), was guilty also of both monetary inflation (a means of governmental theft) and product debasement (a means of commercial theft). By adding a measure of dross to the silver coinage, the actual number of silver coins minted from a given weight of silver could be fraudulently increased. By cutting fine wine with water, the total volume output of wine could be increased, while the actual quality of each unit sold would be diminished. Undoubtedly, these were literal crimes actually being committed. But they also served as figurative symbols for the debasement of the moral and spiritual character of Israel in that day. It is at the least ironic that the only biblical reference to water diluted wine is in a context of rebuke!

Scripture Index

Only those Scripture verses which have a direct reference to alcoholic beverages are included in this index.